|| Brahma Sutras ||

GRAPEVINE INDIA

Published by

GRAPEVINE INDIA PUBLISHERS PVT LTD

www.grapevineindia.com

Delhi | Mumbai

email: grapevineindiapublishers@gmail.com

Ordering Information:

Quantity sales: Special discounts are available on quantity

purchases by corporations, associations, and others.

For details, reach out to the publisher.

First published by Grapevine India 2025

Copyright © Grapevine 2025

All rights reserved

CONTENTS

CHAPTER IV
PHALA ADHYAYA

CHAPTER 1

SECTION 1

(SUTRAS 1-31)

1.1.1 अथातो ब्रह्मजिज्ञासा (Athāto Brahmajijñāsā)

Now, therefore, the inquiry into Brahman.

Atha: Now (an auspicious beginning)
Brahma: The ultimate reality or the absolute
Jijñāsā: Desire for knowledge or inquiry

This sutra introduces the purpose of the text—to explore and understand Brahman. The word "now" implies readiness after acquiring foundational knowledge and qualifications. It signals the start of a profound inquiry into the essence of existence.

1.1.2 जन्माद्यस्य यतः (Janmādyasya Yataḥ)

(Brahman is) that from which the origin, sustenance, and dissolution of this world proceed.

Janma: Creation or origin
Adi: Beginning, middle, and end
Yatah: From which

Brahman is identified as the source, sustainer, and end of the universe. It establishes Brahman as the cause of everything, emphasizing that the material and efficient causes of creation are rooted in Brahman.

1.1.3 शास्त्रयोनित्वात् (ŚāStrayonitvāt)

**(Brahman is known) because
it is the source of the scriptures.**

Śāstra: Scriptures
Yoni: Source or cause
Tvat: Because

Brahman is the source of the knowledge revealed in the Vedas and Upanishads. Since the scriptures originate from Brahman, they guide us to understand its nature.

———— · ◆ · ————

1.1.4 तत्तु समन्वयात् (Tattu Samanvayāt)

**That (Brahman) is to be understood
as consistent with the Upanishads.**

Tat: That (referring to Brahman)
Samanvayāt: Consistency, harmony

The teachings of the Upanishads consistently point to Brahman as the ultimate reality. This sutra highlights that Brahman is the unified subject of all scriptural teachings.

1.1.5 ईक्षतेर्नाशब्दम् (Ikṣater Na Aśabdam)

**Brahman is not unmanifest because
the scriptures declare that It thinks.**

Ikṣate: Thinks or wills
Na: Not
Aśabdam: Without words or sound

Brahman is a conscious being, not merely an abstract principle. The scriptures describe Brahman as having a will or intention, reinforcing its personal and dynamic nature.

———— · ♦ · ————

1.1.6 गौणश्चेन्नात्मशब्दात् (Gauṇaś Cennātmaśabdāt)

**If (Brahman is taken as) secondary,
(it is not correct) because of the term 'Self.'**

Gauṇa: Secondary, metaphorical
Ātmaśabda: The word "Self"

Brahman cannot be understood as a secondary entity because its directly referred to as the Self (Ātman), the core essence of all beings, in the Upanishads.

1.1.7 अन्तःप्रज्ञारुपं तु कर्माद्विवक्षेत्वात्
(Antaḥprajñārūpam Tu Karmādvivakṣetvāt)

(The inner consciousness) as (associated with actions) is intended (because of context).

Antaḥ: Inner or internal
Prajñā: Consciousness or awareness
Rūpam: Form or nature
Tu: However or indeed
Karma: Action or deed
Vivakṣā: Intention or purpose (of expression)
Tvat: Because of

This sutra asserts that Brahman's nature is understood through its inner essence and connection to actions or results, as described in certain contexts.

1.1.8 हेतुमद्भिरभेदात् (Hetumadbhir Abhedāt)

(Brahman is established) because of non-difference (with the cause) as stated in the scriptures with reasons.

Hetumadbhih: With reasons
Abhedāt: Non-difference

The scriptures describe Brahman as non-different from the universe, using reasoning to support this idea. This sutra reinforces that Brahman is both the material and efficient cause of the cosmos.

1.1.9 स्वशब्दात् (Svaśabdāt)

**(Brahman is known) from
its own term in the scriptures.**

Sva: Own
Śabdāt: From the term or word

The Upanishads directly use terms like Brahman and Ātman
to refer to the ultimate reality, leaving no doubt about its identity.
This self-reference affirms Brahman's nature.

* * *

1.1.10 स्मृत्यनवकाशदोषप्रसङ्गः (Smṛtyanavakāśadoṣaprasangaḥ)

**Otherwise, there would be the defect of
scriptures (like Smtis) losing their authority.**

Smṛti: Secondary scriptures or texts
Anavakāśa: No room or space
Doṣa: Defect

If Brahman were not the ultimate cause, it would lead to contradictions
and render the authority of scriptures meaningless. This sutra affirms
Brahman as the basis of all scriptural truths.

1.1.11 तदन्यत्वमरणीयत्वादि विशेषणं तु गुनसामान्यवत्त्वात्
(Tad Anyatvam Araṇīyatvādi Viśeṣaṇaṃ Tu Guṇasāmānyavattvāt)

**The distinctions (like smallness) are only
indicative of attributes and not of essential nature.**

Tad: That (referring to Brahman)
Araṇīyatva: Smallness or minuteness
Viśeṣaṇa: Distinction or quality

Descriptions like smallness (minute as a grain) in the Upanishads are not literal but are used to explain Brahman's subtle nature in a relatable way.

—— • ◆ • ——

1.1.12 आक्षिप्तव्यपदेशात् सैव हि स्थिति: ।
(Ākṣiptavyapadeśāt Saiva Hi Sthitiḥ)

**It is so because the scriptures
declare it through indirect statements.**

Ākṣipta: Indirect or implied
Vyapadeśa: Declaration or mention

The Upanishads sometimes use indirect descriptions to reveal Brahman's characteristics. These should be interpreted with the deeper context of its teachings.

1.1.13 अन्यत्वं तु गुनानां। (Anyatvaṃ Tu Gunānāṃ)

**The attributes (like grossness or minuteness)
are distinct from Brahman itself.**

Anyatva: Otherness or distinction
Gunānām: Of the attributes

Qualities like grossness or minuteness are properties of objects
and not of Brahman, which transcends all such attributes.

1.1.14 तात्त्विकं च गुनयुगपदेशात। (Tāttvikaṃ Ca Guṇayugapadeśāt)

**(These qualities) are also real
because of their simultaneous mention.**

Tāttvika Real or essential
Guṇa: Qualities
Yugapadeśa: Simultaneous mention

When the scriptures mention Brahman along with qualities,
they do so to explain how Brahman interacts with the world,
though Brahman itself remains beyond attributes.

1.1.15 प्रतीयमानत्वाच्य। (Pratīyamānatvācca)

**(The attributes are) inferred because
they are perceived in Brahman's manifestations.**

Pratīyamāna: Perceived
Tvat: Because

The observable qualities in the universe are manifestations of Brahman.
These attributes help us understand its creative power, though Brahman
itself is beyond them.

— ◆ —

1.1.16 विकल्पं च प्रतिपद्यते। (Vikalpaṃ Ca Pratipadyate)

**(The descriptions of Brahman) allow
for alternatives or different viewpoints.**

Vikalpa: Alternatives or variations
Pratipadyate: Are understood

The Upanishads often describe Brahman in various ways to guide
seekers with different levels of understanding. These alternatives are not
contradictions but complementary perspectives.

1.1.17 भेदव्यपदेशान्न ꣵ (Bhedavyapadeśānna)

(Brahman cannot have qualities) because the scriptures do not declare any real distinction.

Bheda: Distinction or difference
Vyapadeśa: Declaration

The Upanishads explicitly teach the oneness of Brahman,
negating any real distinctions or separations within it.

1.1.18 न चान्यत्वं ततः ꣵ (Na Cānyatvaṃ Tataḥ)

Brahman is not different from the universe.

Na: Not.
Anyatva: Otherness
Tataḥ: From that

Brahman is both the material and efficient cause of the universe.
It is not separate from creation but is its very essence, underlying
all forms and phenomena.

1.1.19 स्मरन्ति च (Smaranti Ca)

And (this is also) remembered in the Smtis.

Smaranti: Remember or mention (in Smṛtis)
Ca: And

This sutra states that the Smṛtis (secondary scriptures) also affirm that Brahman is the cause of the universe, corroborating the teachings of the Upanishads.

—————— • ◆ • ——————

1.1.20 अर्थप्रधानं तदुपलब्धेः (Arthapradhānaṃ Tadupalabdheḥ)

The purpose (of scriptural statements) is primarily to reveal Brahman.

Artha: Purpose or meaning
Pradhānaṃ: Primary or main
Tadupalabdheḥ: For the attainment of that (Brahman)

The main objective of the scriptures is to guide seekers to realize Brahman. All descriptions and narratives in the texts serve this ultimate purpose.

1.1.21 उपदेशभेदान्नामधेयवद्वा (Upadeśabhedān Nāmadheyavad Vā)

(Brahman is not different from the world) because of differences in instruction, like names.

Upadeśa: Instruction or teaching
Bheda: Differences
Nāmadheya: Name or designation
Vā: Or

The differences seen in scriptural teachings are similar to different names for the same object. They do not indicate any real distinctions within Brahman.

1.1.22 क्षणिकत्वं परिवर्तनात् (Kṣaṇikatvaṃ Parivartanāt)

(The qualities of Brahman) appear momentary due to transformation.

Kṣaṇikatvaṃ: Momentariness or impermanence
Parivartanāt: Due to change or transformation

Brahman itself is changeless, but its manifestations in the world may appear momentary due to the transformations of its creative power (Māyā).

1.1.23 जगद्व्यापारवचनात् (Jagadvyāpāravacanāt)

(Brahman is the cause) because the scriptures speak of the operation of the universe.

Jagat: Universe or world.
Vyāpāra: Operation or activity
Vacanāt: Because of statement

The scriptures explicitly describe Brahman as the driving force behind the universe's creation, maintenance, and dissolution, establishing it as the ultimate cause.

1.1.24 अस्य च व्याख्यानं प्रविभक्तं च न भेदात्
(Asya Ca Vyākhyānaṃ Pravibhaktaṃ Ca Na Bhedāt)

Its explanation is diverse, yet there is no contradiction due to non-difference.

Asya: Of this (Brahman)
Vyākhyānaṃ: Explanation
Pravibhaktaṃ: Diverse or divided
Bheda: Difference

Although the scriptures describe Brahman in various ways, these descriptions do not create any real division. They reflect the same ultimate reality from different perspectives.

1.1.25 न कर्माविभागादिति चेन्नानादिभेदात्
(Na Karmāvibhāgād Iti Cennānādibhedāt)

**(Brahman is not) due to non-difference
in actions, because of variety in origins.**

Karma: Actions
Avibhāga: Non-difference
Nāna: Diversity or variety
Bheda: Difference

Brahman's nature is not confined to actions or their results. The diversity seen in the world points to Brahman's creative power, not to separateness.

————— • ♦ • —————

1.1.26 असंभवात् (Asambhavāt)

**Because it is impossible
(for Brahman to be different).**

Asambhava: Impossibility or non-occurrence

Brahman cannot be separate from the world because it is the material and efficient cause. Such separation is logically and scripturally untenable.

1.1.27 इतरेषामपि एवमासन्नायाम् (Itareṣām Api Evamāsannāyām)

The same reasoning applies to others (secondary causes) as well.

Itareṣām: Of others
Api: Also
Evam: In this manner
Āsannāyām: Nearness or proximity

Just as Brahman is established as the ultimate cause, other entities like individual souls or nature cannot independently create the universe. Their connection to Brahman is essential.

———— • ◆ • ————

1.1.28 न च प्रमाणान्तरं क्रियायाम् (Na Ca Pramāṇāntaraṃ Kriyāyām)

Nor is there another proof in regard to action.

Na: Not.
Pramāṇa: Proof or evidence
Antara: Another or separate
Kriyā: Action

The existence of Brahman as the cause is adequately proven by the scriptures. There is no need for other means of proof concerning its connection with actions.

1.1.29 न स्वभावत्वम्, प्रकरणात् (Na Svabhāvatvam, Prakaraṇāt)

Not due to mere nature, because of the context.

Na: Not.
Svabhāva: Mere nature or inherent quality
Prakaraṇa: Context

The universe's existence and operation cannot be attributed to mere inherent nature. The scriptures point out Brahman as the conscious and purposeful cause, beyond mere natural occurrence.

———————— • ◆ • ————————

1.1.30 ईक्षतेर्नाशब्दम् (Īkṣater Nāśabdam)

(Brahman is the cause) because of the mention of seeing, and not merely non-sentient (not ascribed to inanimate objects).

Īkṣateḥ: From the term "seeing"
(implying conscious deliberation)
Na: Not
Aśabdam: Not sound, or not applicable
to inanimate objects

The Upanishads describe Brahman as Īkṣate (that which "sees" or deliberates), indicating consciousness and intention. This sutra refutes the notion that the universe arises from unconscious entities, establishing Brahman as the sentient and intelligent cause.

1.1.31 गौणश्चेन्नात्मशब्दात् (Gauṇaś Cennātmaśabdāt)

If it is said to be metaphorical, it is not so, because of the use of the word tman (Self).

Gauṇaḥ: Metaphorical or secondary
Chet: If
Na: Not
Ātmaśabdāt: Because of the use of the term "Self"

The term Ātman is used to refer to Brahman, not metaphorically but literally, as the essential self of all beings. This sutra rejects interpretations that downplay Brahman's role as the ultimate, conscious reality. It emphasizes that Brahman is the true Self, directly identified with the essence of existence.

SECTION 2

(SUTRAS 32-63)

1.2.32 – असत्कल्पत्वान्न संभवः:(Asatkalpatvān Na Sambhavaḥ)

**Creation from non-being
is not possible because it is like a non-entity.**

Asatkalpa: Like non-being or non-existent
Na: Not
Sambhavaḥ: Possibility

The universe cannot arise from non-being (asat), as something cannot come from nothing. This sutra negates the idea of creation being rooted in a void or absence.

———— • ♦ • ————

1.2.33 – उभयत्वावधारणात् (Ubhayatvāvadhāraṇāt)

**(The nature of creation is determined)
by establishing both (cause and effect).**

Ubhayatva: Both (cause and effect)
Avadhāraṇāt: Determined or established

The scriptures describe Brahman as the cause and the universe as its effect. This dual affirmation reinforces the relationship between Brahman and creation.

1.2.34 – कारणत्वादिति चेत् न कर्मविभागादिभ्यः
(Kāraṇatvād Iti Cet Na Karmavibhāgādibhyah)

If (it is argued) that Brahman is the cause, it is not so due to distinctions in actions.

Kāraṇatva: Causality
Iti Cet: If it is said
Na: Not
Karmavibhāga: Division of actions

This sutra addresses objections that Brahman cannot be the cause due to apparent distinctions in actions and effects, explaining that these differences arise from limiting adjuncts (upādhis), not Brahman itself.

1.2.35 – कारणग्रहणात् (Kāraṇagrahaṇāt)

Because the cause (Brahman) is apprehended (in the scriptures).

Kāraṇa: Cause
Grahṇa: Apprehension or recognition

Brahman is recognized as the ultimate cause in the Upanishads. Its presence as the source of all creation is explicitly mentioned.

1.2.36 – समाकरणात् (Samākaraṇāt)

(Creation is possible) because of the combination (of cause and effect).

Samākaraṇa: Combination or connection

The scriptures describe creation as the manifestation of Brahman's potential, where the cause (Brahman) and the effect (the universe) are interconnected.

1.2.37 – नाश्रयत्वं अन्तरभवात् (Nāśrayatvaṃ Antarabhavāt)

(Brahman does not depend on anything) because it exists within all.

Nāśrayatvam: Non-dependence
Antarabhava: Inner existence

Brahman is self-existent and does not rely on anything external, as it resides within all beings as their inner essence.

1.2.38 – विप्रतिषेधाच्च (Vipratiṣedhāc Ca)

And because contradictions (in other theories) are avoided.

Vipratiṣedha: Contradiction
Ca: And

Brahman's status as the ultimate cause resolves contradictions present in other theories of creation, such as materialism or nihilism.

———— ·◆· ————

1.2.39 – संभवाच्च योनौ (Sambhavāc Ca Yonau)

And (creation is possible) because of its origin in Brahman.

Sambhava: Possibility or emergence
Yoni: Source or womb

The scriptures describe Brahman as the source of all creation, making the emergence of the universe logical and intelligible.

1.2.40 – स्थानाधिकरणत्वाच्च (Sthānādhikaraṇatvāc Ca)

And because (Brahman) is the substratum of existence.

Sthāna: Place or position
Adhikaraṇatva: Being the substratum

Brahman serves as the foundation for all existence,
much like a substratum supports its superimpositions.

1.2.41 – न शक्तिघातोऽन्यथानुपपत्ते:(Na Śaktighāto'nyathānupapatteḥ)

There is no destruction of power,
as otherwise creation would not be possible.

Śaktighāta: Destruction of power
Anya: Otherwise
Anupapatteḥ: Non-possibility

The power of Brahman (Māyā) to create the universe is not
negated, as creation would otherwise become inexplicable.

1.2.42 – साक्षादप्यविशेषात् (Sākṣād Apyaviśeṣāt)

Even directly, there is no distinction (between Brahman and the universe).

Sākṣāt: Directly
Aviśeṣāt: Due to non-distinction

Brahman is directly identified with the universe in
the scriptures, demonstrating their unity without distinctions.

1.2.43 – अशक्याश्रयत्वान्न शून्यम् (Aśakyāśrayatvān Na Śūnyam)

(The ultimate cause) cannot be void, because it cannot serve as a basis.

Aśakya: Impossible
Āśrayatva: Basis or support
Na: Not
Śūnyam: Void or emptiness

This sutra rejects the theory that creation arises from void or emptiness
(śūnya). Emptiness cannot act as a basis or support for the universe.

1.2.44 – तदनपेक्षत्वादिति चेत् न अधिष्ठानं तदुपलब्धेः
(Tadanapekṣatvād Iti Cet Na Adhiṣṭhānaṃ Tadupalabdheḥ)

If it is argued that (a basis) is not needed,
it is not so, because the substratum is apprehended.

Tad Anapekṣatvāt: Due to not requiring that
Na: Not
Adhiṣṭhānam: Substratum or basis
Tadupalabdheḥ: Because it is apprehended

The universe requires a substratum, which is Brahman. The scriptures directly teach this apprehension of Brahman as the basis of all existence.

1.2.45 – कार्यत्वाच्च अक्षणवत् (Kāryatvāc Ca Akṣaṇavat)

And because it is an effect, like a wheel.

Kāryatvāt: Because of being an effect
Ca: And
Akṣaṇavat: Like a wheel

The universe, being an effect, requires a cause, just as a wheel depends on its hub. This analogy affirms Brahman as the cause.

1.2.46 – न च किंचिद्विषयं व्यतिरेकः (Na Ca Kiṃcid Viṣayaṃ Vyatirekaḥ)

And nothing (exists) apart from the subject (Brahman).

Na: Not
Ca: And
Kiṃcid: Anything
Viṣayaṃ: Subject or object
Vyatirekaḥ: Separation

Brahman is the ultimate reality, and nothing
exists independently of it. All phenomena are its manifestations.

* ◆ *

1.2.47 – अशुद्धमिति चेत् न शौचात् (Aśuddham Iti Cet Na Śaucāt)

If it is argued that it is impure,
it is not so, because of its purity.

Aśuddham: Impure
Iti Cet: If it is said
Na: Not
Śaucāt: Because of purity

Brahman is pure by nature, free from defects
and impurities. Any perceived impurity arises from ignorance.

1.2.48 – तथाच दर्शयति (Tathā Ca Darśayati)

And thus the scripture shows.

Tathā: Thus
Ca: And
Darśayati: Shows or teaches

The scriptures confirm Brahman's purity and transcendence, making it the suitable cause of the universe.

———— • ◆ • ————

1.2.49 – अप्रत्यये न ह्यनुमानं विशेषात्
(Apratyaye Na Hyanumānam Viśeṣāt)

In the absence of direct perception, inference does not apply, due to specificity.

Apratyaye: In the absence of direct perception.
Na: Not
Hi: Certainly
Anumānam: Inference
Viśeṣāt: Due to specificity

Brahman cannot be inferred from logic alone, as its nature is specific and beyond sensory perception. It is apprehended through scripture.

1.2.50 – इक्षत्यभिसंधानात् (Ikṣatyabhisaṃdhānāt)

Because it is deliberated upon as the seer.

Ikṣati: Sees or deliberates
Abhisaṃdhānāt: Due to contemplation

Brahman is described as the seer and conscious
agent in creation. This deliberation confirms its sentient nature.

— ◆ ◆ —

1.2.51 – सत्यर्थत्वेन चाभ्यासात् (Sattyarthatvena Cābhyāsāt)

And also because of its repeated description as existence.

Sattyarthatvena: As pure existence
Ca: And
Abhyāsāt: Repeatedly or consistently

The scriptures consistently describe Brahman as pure
existence (Sat), reinforcing its role as the foundational reality.

1.2.52 – प्रकृतिश्च प्रतीयेत नित्यत्वात् (Prakṛtiś Ca Pratīyeta Nityatvāt)

And Prakriti (nature) is also recognized as eternal.

Prakṛti: Nature
Pratīyeta: Is recognized
Nityatvāt: Because of being eternal

Prakriti (nature) functions as the material cause of the universe but operates under Brahman's guidance. Brahman's eternity ensures the continuity of creation.

————— · ♦ · —————

1.2.53 – गुणव्यपदेशाच्च (Guṇavyapadeśāc Ca)

And because of the mention of attributes.

Guṇa: Attribute
Vyapadeśāt: Mention or statement
Ca: And

The scriptures describe Brahman's attributes, such as omniscience and omnipotence, confirming its role as the ultimate cause.

1.2.54 – असतोऽभावादिति चेत् न धर्मान्तरत्वात्
(Asato'bhāvād Iti Cet Na Dharmāntaratvāt)

**If it is argued that the unreal has no existence,
it is not so, because of its distinct nature.**

Asataḥ: Of the unreal
Abhāvāt: Absence
Iti Cet: If it is said
Na: Not
Dharmāntaratvāt: Due to distinct nature

Brahman's manifestation as the universe does not negate
its essential reality. The universe is distinct as an
effect but rooted in Brahman.

1.2.55 – प्रपञ्चश्च वस्तुशब्दात् (Prapañcaś Ca Vastuśabdāt)

**And the universe is denoted by
the term "reality" (or substance).**

Prapañca: Universe or creation
Ca: And
Vastu: Reality or substance
Śabdāt: Due to the word

The word "reality" (Vastu) refers to the totality of creation, reinforcing
that the universe is real, though dependent on Brahman for its existence.

1.2.56 – कर्तृत्वेन च (Kartṛtvena Ca)

And because of its role as the doer.

Kartṛtva: The state of being the doer or agent
Ca: And

Brahman is the ultimate doer, as it is the agent responsible for the actions within the universe. All activities are manifestations of its will.

1.2.57 – तदर्थवशाद्व्यक्तिरुपाधिन्यायात्
(Tadarthavaśād Vyaktir Upādhinnyāyāt)

**The manifestation occurs due to
the limitation of the cause (through adjuncts).**

Tadarthavaśāt: Due to the purpose of that (the cause)
Vyakti: Manifestation or expression
Upādhi: Limiting adjunct
Nyāyāt: Due to the analogy or rule

The universe's manifestation is a result of Brahman being limited by adjuncts (upādhis), which allow for the appearance of diversity while retaining its unity.

1.2.58 – निराकारत्वं च निर्बीजत्वादिति चेद्
(Nirākāratvaṃ Ca Nirbījatvād Iti Ched)

**If it is said that Brahman is formless and
without seed, it is not so, due to its being the source of all.**

Nirākāratva: Formlessness
Ca: And
Nirbījatvāt: Without seed
Iti Cet: If it is said

While Brahman is formless, it is also the source of all forms and entities.
It transcends form but contains the potential for all manifestations.

———— • ◆ • ————

1.2.59 – कार्यविशेषेण निरवस्थात् (Kāryaviśeṣeṇa Niravasthāt)

**Brahman is without limitation,
as it is not subject to specific effects.**

Kāryaviśeṣeṇa: Due to the specificity of effects
Niravasthāt: Without limitation

Brahman is free from limitations and does not undergo
any transformation, as it is the cause of all transformations.

1.2.60 – कारणे च निरवस्थात् (Kāraṇe Ca Niravasthāt)

The cause (Brahman) is also without limitation.

Kāraṇe: In the cause
Ca: And
Niravasthāt: Without limitation

Brahman, as the ultimate cause, is not limited by the effects it generates. It remains unaffected and free from any restrictions.

1.2.61 – स्थूलत्वाद्यदृच्छायाम् (Sthūlatvādyadṛcchāyām)

And the grossness of the world (arises) due to its inherent nature of contingency.

Sthūlatva: Grossness or materiality
Adṛcchā: Inherent or spontaneous
Yām: Due to

The material universe, as a gross manifestation, arises due to Brahman's power of manifestation through Māyā (illusion) and contingency.

1.2.62 – नैव तु अर्थनिश्चयाद् (Naiva Tu Arthaniscayād)

But not due to the definitive determination of meaning.

Naiva: Not
Tu: But
Arthaniscaya: Determination of meaning

Brahman, though the cause of the universe, is not limited to any specific meaning or effect. It transcends conceptualization and description.

1.2.63 – न्यायमूलं च दर्शनात् (Nyāyamūlaṃ Ca Darśanāt)

**And because it is the root of all logical
systems, as shown by the scriptures.**

Nyāyamūlam: The root or foundation of logic
Ca: And
Darśanāt: Due to being shown

Brahman is the root and foundation of all logical systems.
The scriptures affirm its role as the source of all reasoning and knowledge.

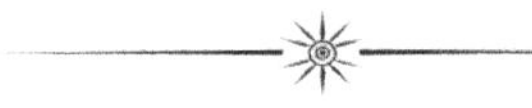

SECTION 3

(SUTRAS 64 - 106)

1.3.64 – आकाशे चीयते (Ākāśe Cīyate)

(Meditation is valid) on space also.

Ākāśe: In space
Cīyate: Is accepted or included

This sutra clarifies that meditation on ākāśa (space), as mentioned in the scriptures, is valid because space represents an aspect of Brahman.

1.3.65 – गुणश्रुतेश्च (Guṇaśruteś Ca)

And because of the mention of qualities.

Guṇa: Quality
Śruteḥ: From the scriptures
Ca: And

Meditation on space is supported by the scripture because qualities like infiniteness are attributed to it, which point to its connection with Brahman.

1.3.66 – वायुवच्चैत्रत्वात् (Vāyuvac Caitreṇatvāt)

(Meditation on space is valid) as it is similar to air.

Vāyu: Air
Caitreṇatvāt: Similarity or analogy

Space is comparable to air, which is also a subtle element
and accepted as an object of meditation in scriptures.

1.3.67 – दृष्टश्रुतोपदेशात् (Dṛṣṭaśrutopadeśāt)

Because of perception and scriptural instruction.

Dṛṣṭa: Seen or perceived
Śruta: Heard (from scripture)
Upadeśāt: Instruction or teaching

Meditation on space is valid because it is perceived
as all-encompassing and is also instructed in the scriptures.

1.3.68 – अन्यत्र च गुह्यं (Anyatra Ca Guhyaṃ)

And the secret (teaching) is elsewhere too.

Anyatra: Elsewhere
Ca: And
Guhyaṃ: Secret

The secret teachings of meditation are also presented in other scriptures, emphasizing its universality and importance.

1.3.69 – तद्गुणसारत्वात् (Tadguṇasāratvāt)

Because of the essence of its qualities.

Tad: That (Brahman)
Guṇa: Qualities
Sāratvāt: Being the essence

The qualities of Brahman, like infiniteness and subtlety, are the essence of space, making it a suitable object for meditation.

1.3.70 – ज्यायस्त्वात्तु (Jyāyastvāt Tu)

**But because of superiority
(Brahman is the ultimate object of meditation).**

Jyāyastvāt: Due to being superior
Tu: But

While space can be meditated upon, Brahman is
superior and should be the ultimate object of focus.

1.3.71 – चक्षुरादिवदविरोधः (Cakṣurādivad Avirodhaḥ)

**There is no contradiction, as in
the case of the eye and other senses.**

Cakṣus: Eye
Ādivat: And others, like
Avirodhaḥ: No contradiction

Just as the senses like the eyes are different but contribute to knowledge,
different objects of meditation complement each other without contradiction.

1.3.72 – शारीरं तु भेदनिवृत्त्या (ŚāRraṃ Tu Bhedanivṛttyā)

(Meditation is possible) on the embodied self by the cessation of differences.

Śārīram: Related to the body or self
Tu: But
Bhedanivṛttyā: By removing distinctions

Meditation on the individual self is possible when distinctions between the self and Brahman are resolved.

1.3.73 – शुद्धोपदेशात् (ŚUddhopadeśāt)

Because of the teaching of purity.

Śuddha: Pure
Upadeśāt: Due to instruction

Scriptures teach the purity of the self, aligning it with Brahman and making it a valid subject of meditation.

1.3.74 – नैतरेषां अविरोधः (Naitareṣāṃ Avirodhaḥ)

There is no contradiction regarding others.

Na: Not
Itareṣām: Of others
Avirodhaḥ: No contradiction

Other forms of meditation do not contradict meditation
on Brahman; they complement and lead to the same realization.

———— • ♦ • ————

1.3.75 – तत्त्वमसिवदविरोधः (Tattvamasi Vad Avirodhaḥ)

There is no contradiction,
as in the case of "Tat Tvam Asi" (That Thou Art).

Tat Tvam Asi: That Thou Art
Vad: As in
Avirodhaḥ: No contradiction

Just as the Mahāvākya ("great saying") points to non-duality, meditations
on various aspects of Brahman align with the same ultimate truth.

1.3.76 – अन्यथा च श्रुतेः (Anyathā Ca Śruteḥ)

And otherwise (meditation is valid) because of the scriptural statement.

Anyathā: Otherwise
Ca: And
Śruteḥ: From the scriptures

Meditations are validated when scripture provides instructions. Diverse meditations serve the seeker's progress, as described in the Vedas.

1.3.77 – न वा सामान्यवत् (Na Vā Sāmānyavat)

Or not so, as in the case of generality.

Na: Not
Vā: Or
Sāmānyavat: Like generality

Meditation on Brahman cannot be equated with meditations on general objects. Brahman is unique and transcendent, distinct from ordinary entities.

1.3.78 – अपि संयोगात् (Api Saṃyogāt)

Even (meditation is possible) due to association.

Api: Even
Saṃyogāt: Due to association

Meditation can be applied to symbols or representations of Brahman, as their association with Brahman bestows significance.

———— • ◆ • ————

1.3.79 – शब्दाच्च (ŚAbdāc Ca)

And because of the scriptural word.

Śabdāt: From the word (scripture)
Ca: And

Scripture supports symbolic meditations by explicitly mentioning associated attributes and symbols of Brahman.

1.3.80 – आदित्यादिमध्येऽनुपपत्तेः (ĀDityādimadhye'nupapatteḥ)

(Brahman is not limited to) the midst of the sun, etc., as it is unreasonable.

Āditya: Sun
Ādimadhye: Midst of (sun and others)
Anupapatteḥ: Because of unreasonableness

Brahman's omnipresence is not confined to celestial bodies like the sun. Such references are symbolic, not literal.

———— · ◆ · ————

1.3.81 – पर्युपास्यानुगमात् (Paryupāsyānugamāt)

Because (scripture shows) the following of objects to be meditated upon.

Paryupāsya: Objects of meditation
Anugamāt: Due to following

The meditator focuses on Brahman-related symbols, guided by scriptural references, ensuring consistent meditation practices.

1.3.82 – एकेक्षणं गच्छन्ति वचनेनैवम्
(Ekeṣaṇam Gacchanti Vacanenaivam)

**By the scriptural text, (Brahman)
is declared to be one without a second.**

Eka: One
Iṣaṇam: Observation or realization
Vacanena: By the statement
Evam: Thus

Brahman is described as indivisible and non-dual in
the scriptures, highlighting its uniqueness as the ultimate reality.

· ◆ ·

1.3.83 – विशेषणादिति चेत् न, वाक्यशेषात् (Viśeṣaṇāditi Cet Na, Vākyaśeṣāt)

**If it is argued that there is qualification,
(it is) not so, because of the concluding statement.**

Viśeṣaṇa: Qualification
Chet: If
Na: Not
Vākyaśeṣāt: From the concluding portion of the text.

Brahman's descriptions in the scriptures are not limiting qualifiers but
pointers to its infinite nature. The conclusions affirm its transcendence.

1.3.84 – आश्रयवन्नोपपत्तेः (Āśrayavan Nopapatteḥ)

(Meditation on Brahman) is not reasonable if based on support.

Āśrayavan: Having a support
Na: Not
Upapatteḥ: Reasonableness

Brahman is self-sufficient and does not depend on external supports or loci for meditation or realization.

———— • ◆ • ————

1.3.85 – प्रधानाधीनत्वं तु विभक्तेष्वेव (Pradhānādhīnatvaṃ Tu Vibhakteṣveva)

Dependence on the main (Brahman) applies only to the differentiated.

Pradhānādhīnatvam: Dependence on the principal
Tu: But
Vibhakteṣv: In the differentiated
Eva: Only

Differentiated entities depend on Brahman,
but Brahman itself is independent and indivisible.

1.3.86 – उपदेशाद्विशेषणं (Upadeśādviśeṣaṇaṃ)

Qualification arises from instruction.

Upadeśāt: From teaching or instruction
Viśeṣaṇam: Qualification or specification

Scriptural instructions introduce distinctions for
meditation purposes but do not limit Brahman's essence.

———— • ♦ • ————

1.3.87 – न सविकल्पमविशेषात् (Na Savikalpam Aviśeṣāt)

Not with distinctions, because there is no difference.

Na: Not
Savikalpam: With distinctions
Aviśeṣāt: Due to non-difference

Brahman is indivisible and beyond distinctions,
even though scriptures sometimes use them for instructional clarity.

1.3.88 – अन्तरात्मशब्दादिति चेत् न आत्मन्युपलम्भात्
(Antarātmaśabdāditi Cet Na Ātmanyupalambhāt)

If it is argued that the word "inner self" implies distinction, it is not so, because it refers to the self.

Antarātma: Inner self
Śabdāt: From the word
Chet: If
Na: Not
Ātmanyupalambhāt: Perception as the self

The term "inner self" indicates Brahman as the essence of all beings, not a separate or distinct entity.

1.3.89 – तद्यथाऽसङ्गो ह्यायतनं बुद्धिर्यथा
(Tadyathā'saṅgo Hyāyatanaṃ Buddhiryathā)

As (the self is) unattached, so is the basis of intelligence.

Tadyathā: As
Asaṅgaḥ: Unattached
Āyatanaṃ: Basis
Buddhiḥ: Intelligence

The self is free from attachment, serving as the substratum for all intelligence, and aligns with Brahman's essence.

1.3.90 – नात्मोपसंवरणात् (Nātmopasaṃvaraṇāt)

Not (possible), because the self is not enclosed.

Na: Not
Ātma: Self
Upasaṃvaraṇāt: Enclosure or confinement

Brahman, being infinite, cannot be confined
or enclosed within anything, emphasizing its boundless nature.

·◆·

1.3.91 – विभक्तस्यैव च गुणश्रुतेः
(Vibhaktasyaiva Ca Guṇaśruteḥ)

And only for the differentiated, because of the mention of qualities.

Vibhaktasya: Differentiated
Ca: And
Guṇa: Qualities
Śruteḥ: From the scriptures

Scriptural references to qualities apply only to the differentiated aspects of existence, not to the ultimate Brahman, which is beyond all qualities.

1.3.92 – सत्त्वाधिकारः सन्देहविशेषविज्ञानात्तु
(Sattvādhikāraḥ Sandehaviśeṣavijñānāttu)

(Meditation on Brahman) is directed to the existent, as it is known to resolve doubts.

Sattva: Existence
Adhikāraḥ: Instruction or entitlement
Sandeha: Doubt
Viśeṣa: Special
Vijñānāt: Due to knowledge

Meditations prescribed by scriptures focus on Brahman's existence, providing clarity and resolving doubts about ultimate reality.

* ◆ *

1.3.93 – सर्वसामान्यं नैतरेषाम् (Sarvasāmānyaṁ Naitareṣām)

The general statement does not apply to other cases.

Sarva: All
Sāmānyaṁ: Generality
Na: Not
Itareṣām: Of others

General scriptural references to meditations are specific to certain contexts and do not universally apply to all situations.

1.3.94 – ज्ञप्तेश्चाधिकरणस्याचित्रता (Jñapteś Cādhikaraṇasyācitratā)

**And because of the teaching of consciousness,
the subject (Brahman) is not diverse.**

Jñapteḥ: Of knowledge or consciousness
Adhikaraṇasya: Of the subject
Acitratā: Non-diversity

Brahman, being pure consciousness, is non-dual
and indivisible, contrary to the appearance of diversity.

———— • ◆ • ————

1.3.95 – ज्ञानवदविरोधः (Jñānavad Avirodhaḥ)

**(Meditation on Brahman is valid) as in
the case of knowledge, with no contradiction.**

Jñānavat: Like knowledge
Avirodhaḥ: Without contradiction

Just as knowledge does not contradict itself, meditations
on Brahman, despite varying forms, align with its singular nature.

1.3.96 – स्वरूपोपदेशात्तु (Svarūpopadeśāt Tu)

But because of the instruction about its essential nature.

Svarūpa: Essential nature
Upadeśāt: Due to teaching
Tu: But

Brahman's meditations focus on its essential, intrinsic
nature as taught in the scriptures, reinforcing its ultimate reality.

———— • ♦ • ————

1.3.97 – सती हि स्थितिर्बहिरध्यानन्यायेन
(Satī Hi Sthitir Bahir Adhyānanyāyena)

**The existent Brahman remains valid by
the reasoning of external meditation.**

Satī: Existence
Sthitiḥ: State or existence
Bahir: External
Adhyāna: Meditation
Nyāyena: By reasoning

Meditation on Brahman through external objects is acceptable
provided it aligns with logical reasoning and scriptural intent.

1.3.98 – अप्राप्तिरुपलक्षणम् (Aprāptir Upalakṣaṇam)

Non-attainment is indicative (of something higher).

Aprāptiḥ: Non-attainment
Upalakṣaṇam: Indicative

The inability to fully comprehend Brahman indicates its transcendence and serves as a reminder of its infinite nature.

——————— · ◆ · ———————

1.3.99 – स्वातन्त्र्याच्च तद्यथा (Svātantryāc Ca Tadyathā)

And because of independence, as stated.

Svātantryāt: Due to independence
Ca: And
Tadyathā: As stated

Brahman's independence affirms its supreme nature, which is highlighted in scriptural descriptions.

1.3.100 – कारणात् चैतन्यं हि (Kāraṇāt Caitanyaṃ Hi)

Because of its causality, it is consciousness indeed.

Kāraṇāt: Due to being the cause
Caitanyaṃ: Consciousness.
Hi: Indeed

Brahman is described as pure consciousness
because it is the cause of the universe and all beings.

———— • ◆ • ————

1.3.101 – सर्वप्रत्ययसंविदः स्वभावतस्तु
(Sarvapratyayasaṃvidaḥ Svabhāvatas Tu)

But it is the consciousness of all mental states, by nature.

Sarva: All
Pratyaya: Cognitions or thoughts
Saṃvidaḥ: Consciousness
Svabhāvataḥ: By nature

Brahman's nature is the universal awareness that
illuminates all individual thoughts and experiences.

1.3.102 – एकत्वान्न विभक्तमित्येकवाक्यम्
(Ekatvānna Vibhaktam Ityekavākyam)

Because of unity, it is not divided, as the text declares.

Ekatvāt: Due to unity
Na: Not
Vibhaktam: Divided
Ityekavākyam: Thus is the single statement

Brahman's unity is affirmed by scriptural statements,
rejecting any notion of division or duality.

1.3.103 – तदनन्यत्वं दर्शयति (Tadananatvaṃ Darśayati)

(The scripture) shows its non-difference.

Tad: That
Ananyatvaṃ: Non-difference
Darśayati: Shows

Scriptures reveal the essential non-difference between the
individual self and Brahman, affirming Advaita (non-duality).

1.3.104 – श्रुतेः सर्वमालम्ब्य तद्भक्तित्वात्तु
(ŚShruteḥ Sarvamālambya Tadbhaktitvāttu)

**Because the scripture teaches everything
as dependent on it, being dedicated to it.**

Śruteḥ: From scripture
Sarvam: Everything
Ālambya: Dependent on
Tadbhaktitvāt: Due to being dedicated to it
Tu: But

Scriptures present everything as dependent on Brahman,
demonstrating its supreme and inclusive nature.

———— • ◆ • ————

1.3.105 – आत्मनश्च परामर्शः (ĀAtmanaś Ca Parāmarśaḥ)

And there is reference to the self (in the scriptures).

Ātmanaḥ: Of the self
Ca: And
Parāmarśaḥ: Reference or consideration

This sutra emphasizes that the Upanishads refer to
the self (Ātman) in discussions about Brahman, highlighting
the oneness of Ātman and Brahman in scriptural teachings.

1.3.106 – भेदव्यपदेशाच्य (Bhedavyapadeśāc Ca)

And because of the declaration of difference (in the scriptures).

Bheda: Difference
Vyapadeśāt: Declaration or mention
Ca: And

While the ultimate reality is non-dual, scriptures also
describe apparent differences to guide seekers at various levels of
understanding, accommodating diverse spiritual capacities.

SECTION 4

(SUTRAS 107 - 134)

1.4.107 – अनुवृत्तेराश्रयणात् (Anuvrtter Āsrayaṇāt)

(The qualities of Brahman are established) because they are repeatedly declared and are supported (by the scriptures).

Anuvrtteḥ: Repetition or continuity.
Āsrayaṇāt: Being supported.

The qualities of Brahman, like omniscience and omnipotence, are consistently mentioned in scriptures, affirming their validity and connection with the ultimate reality.

———— • ♦ • ————

1.4.108 – साक्षाच्चोभयाम्नानात् (Sākṣāc Cobhayāmnānāt)

(These qualities are established) because of their direct mention in both ways.

Sākṣāt: Directly.
Ca: And.
Ubhayāmnānāt: From both mentions (positive and negative aspects).

Brahman is described in scriptures through both positive attributes (e.g., knowledge and bliss) and negations (e.g., beyond name and form), ensuring clarity about its nature.

1.4.109 – कारणत्वाच्च शास्त्रस्य (Kāraṇatvācca Śāstrasya)

And because the scriptures are the cause
(of the knowledge of Brahman).

Kāraṇatvāt: Being the cause.
Ca: And.
Śāstrasya: Of the scriptures.

Explanation: Scriptures are the ultimate authority in imparting knowledge about Brahman, which cannot be known through other means like perception or inference.

———— ∙♦∙ ————

1.4.110 – गुणाधिक्यं तूत्तरेषाम् (Guṇādhikyaṃ Tūttareṣām)

But the higher qualities
(belong to Brahman) in comparison to others (beings).

Guṇa: Qualities.
Ādhikyam: Superiority.
Tu: But.
Uttareṣām: Of the higher.

The supreme qualities of Brahman, such as infinity and perfection, surpass those of any created being, including gods or celestial entities.

1.4.111 – यथाश्रयभवोऽन्यत्र तथोपदेशात्
(Yathāśrayabhavo'nyatra Tathopadeśāt)

As the qualities depend on their substratum, so is it taught elsewhere.

Yathā: As.
Āśrayabhavaḥ: Dependent on the substratum.
Anyatra: Elsewhere.
Tathā: So.
Upadeśāt: As taught.

The qualities of Brahman, such as bliss and knowledge, are inseparable from its substratum, aligning with teachings found in other contexts.

———— · ◆ · ————

1.4.112 – उपक्रमोपसंहाराभ्यां विशेषितत्वात्
(Upakramopasaṃhārābhyāṃ Viśeṣitatvāt)

Because of specification through the beginning and conclusion.

Upakrama: Beginning.
Upasaṃhāra: Conclusion.
Viśeṣitatvāt: Specificity.

The consistent mention of Brahman at the start and end of scriptural discussions emphasizes its centrality and supreme nature.

1.4.113 – कारणग्रहणाच्य (Kāraṇagrahaṇācca)

And because (Brahman is) understood as the cause.

Kāraṇa: Cause.
Grahṇāt: Understanding.
Ca: And.

Brahman is recognized as the ultimate cause of
the universe, as repeatedly confirmed by scriptural teachings.

1.4.114 – तद्दर्शनात् (Taddarśanāt)

(Brahman is established) because it is seen (in the scriptures).

Tat: That (Brahman).
Darśanāt: Because it is seen.

The direct perception or realization of Brahman is confirmed through
scriptural passages describing such experiences.

1.4.115 – परिणामाच्च (Pariṇāmācca)

And because (the universe is) its transformation.

Pariṇāmaḥ: Transformation.
Ca: And.

The universe is a transformation of Brahman's power, reinforcing its role as the material and efficient cause.

———— • ♦ • ————

1.4.116 – साक्षाच्चोभयाभावः (Sākṣāc Cobhayābhāvaḥ)

And because of the direct absence of both (causes and effects in Brahman).

Sākṣāt: Directly.
Ca: And.
Ubhayābhāvaḥ: Absence of both.

In its purest state, Brahman transcends all causal and effectual limitations, emphasizing its transcendence.

CHAPTER 2

SECTION 1

(SUTRAS 135-171)

2.1.135 – स्मृत्यनवकाशदोषप्रसङ्ग इति चेन्नान्यस्मृत्यनवकाशदोषप्रसङ्गात्
(Smṛtyanavakāśadoṣaprasaṅga Iti
Cennānyasmṛtyanavakāśadoṣaprasaṅgāt)

If it is argued that (the Vedantic doctrine leads to) the defect of leaving no room for other Smtis, it is not so, because the defect would equally apply to other Smtis.

Smṛti: Secondary scriptures or traditional texts
Anavakāśa: Lack of room or opportunity
Doṣa: Defect
Prasaṅga: Possibility or consequence

This sutra refutes the objection that Vedanta invalidates other scriptures. It argues that if Vedanta creates a conflict, the same logic would affect those secondary scriptures themselves.

2.1.136 – प्रत्यक्षानुमानाभ्यामन्यस्मृत्यनवकाशदोषप्रसङ्गः
(Pratyakṣānumānābhyāmanyasmṛtyanavakāśadoṣaprasaṅgaḥ)

The defect of leaving no room for other
Smtis arises even from perception and inference.

Pratyakṣa: Direct perception
Anumāna: Inference
Abhyām: By these two
Anya: Other
Doṣa: Defect

This sutra continues the argument, explaining that even direct perception and inference could render other Smṛtis unnecessary, showing that this is not a unique issue for Vedanta.

— ◆ —

2.1.137 – न चात्र लोकविरुद्धं चेष्टितम् (Na Cātra Lokaviruddhaṃ Ceṣṭitam)

Nor is there anything opposed to
common experience (in this doctrine).

Na: Not
Atra: Here (in Vedanta)
Loka: Worldly or common experience
Viruddham: Contradictory
Ceṣṭitam: Action or doctrine

Vedanta does not contradict worldly experience or practical life. Instead, it complements and explains the ultimate reality beyond perception.

2.1.138 – तत्र प्रमाणं साक्षात् (Tatra Pramāṇaṃ Sākṣāt)

There (in Vedanta), direct testimony (of the Vedas) is the authority.

Tatra: There
Pramāṇaṃ: Authority or means of knowledge
Sākṣāt: Directly

Vedantic truths rely on direct scriptural testimony, which is the most authoritative source for understanding Brahman.

———— •◆• ————

2.1.139 – वेदान्तेषु तद्वचनेन च प्रमाणम् (Vedānteṣu Tadvacanena Ca Pramāṇam)

In the Vedantic texts, the direct words (of the Vedas) are also the authority.

Vedānteṣu: In the Vedantic texts
Tadvacanena: By their words
Ca: And
Pramāṇam: Authority

The direct teachings of the Upanishads and other Vedantic texts serve as the ultimate proof of Brahman's existence and nature.

2.1.140 – समानाधिकरणत्वं च शब्दार्थोपपत्तेः
(Samndhikaraatva Ca abdrthopapatte)

And (there is unity) because of the agreement of the meanings of the words.

Samānādhikaraṇatvaṃ: Unity of reference
Ca: And
Śabda: Words
Artha: Meaning
Upapatteḥ: Logical consistency

The words in the Vedantic texts consistently point
to a single reality, Brahman, through their unified meaning.

2.1.141 – साङ्गत्येन शब्दार्थानां तत्राप्युपपत्तिः
(Sāṅgatvena Śabdārthānāṃ Tatrāpyupapattiḥ)

There is agreement in the meanings of the words in that context as well.

Sāṅgatvena: Consistency or agreement
Śabda: Words
Artha: Meaning
Tatra: There
Api: Also
Upapattiḥ: Reasonableness

The agreement in word meanings further validates
the Vedantic teaching about Brahman's nature and role.

2.1.142 – तत्र सर्वं च प्रमाणम् (Tatra Sarvaṃ Ca Pramāṇam)

There (in Vedanta), everything (is supported) by evidence.

Tatra: There
Sarvaṃ: Everything
Ca: And
Pramāṇam: Proof or evidence

Vedanta is firmly established on evidence from scriptures, logic, and experiential knowledge, leaving no room for contradiction.

2.1.143 – हेतुश्च तत्प्रतिषेधः (Hetuśca Tatpratiṣedhaḥ)

And (the cause of opposition is) the negation of that.

Hetuḥ: Cause
Ca: And
Tat: That
Pratiṣedhaḥ: Negation

The opposition to Vedanta arises due to the denial of its core principles, but such negations are baseless when examined against scriptural evidence.

2.1.144 – तत्रायमर्थोऽविरुद्धः (Tatrāyamartho'viruddhaḥ)

There, this doctrine is free from contradiction.

Tatra: There
Ayam: This
Arthaḥ: Doctrine or meaning
Aviruddhaḥ: Free from contradiction

The teachings of Vedanta are harmonious and logically consistent with scriptural authority, free from conflicts with reason or experience.

———————— • ◆ • ————————

2.1.145 – तथा ह्यनुमानम् (Tathā Hyanumānam)

Because it is so, inference also (supports it).

Tathā: In this way
Hi: Indeed
Anumānam: Inference

This sutra emphasizes that the principles of Vedanta align with logical inference. Reasoning complements the teachings of the scriptures, reinforcing their validity.

2.1.146 – न च शब्दादितः प्रामाण्यम् (Na Ca Śabdāditaḥ Prāmāṇyam)

Nor is validity derived only from words, etc.

Na: Not
Ca: And
Śabda: Words
Āditaḥ: And so on
Prāmāṇyam: Authority or validity

Vedanta's authority is not limited to verbal testimony (scriptures); it also stems from logical coherence and experiential verification.

———— • ◆ • ————

2.1.147 – न च प्रमाणेष्वविरोधः (Na Ca Pramāṇeṣvavirodhaḥ)

Nor is there any contradiction among the sources of knowledge.

Na: Not
Ca: And
Pramāṇeṣu: In the sources of knowledge
Avirodhaḥ: Contradiction

The different means of knowledge—perception, inference, and scriptural testimony—do not conflict with each other but instead complement the Vedantic understanding of Brahman.

2.1.148 – तस्मात्सर्वमविद्विदं प्रामाण्यमिति
(Tasmātsarvamavidvidaṃ Prāmāṇyamiti)

Therefore, all this (is based on) non-contradicted authority.

Tasmāt: Therefore
Sarvam: All
Avidvidaṃ: Non-contradicted
Prāmāṇyam: Authority

Since the teachings of Vedanta harmonize with all valid sources of knowledge, they stand as irrefutable and authoritative.

––––––––– · ♦ · –––––––––

2.1.149 – हेतुभिश्च तत्प्रतिषेधः सम्भवति
(Hetubhiśca Tatpratiṣedhaḥ Sambhavati)

**And through reasoning, the negation
of that (opposition) is possible.**

Hetubhiḥ: Through reasoning
Ca: And
Tat: That
Pratiṣedhaḥ: Negation
Sambhavati: Is possible

Logical reasoning helps refute arguments against Vedanta, proving its consistency and aligning it with scriptural authority.

2.1.150 – तदुक्तं स्मृतिषु स्पष्टं तस्मात् (Taduktaṃ Smṛtiṣu Sphaṣṭaṃ Tasmāt)

That (truth) has been clearly stated in the Smtis.

Tad: That
Uktam: Stated
Smṛtiṣu: In the secondary scriptures
Sphaṣṭam: Clearly
Tasmāt: Therefore

The Smṛtis (secondary scriptures) also clearly affirm
the doctrines of Vedanta, further strengthening its credibility.

·◆·

2.1.151 – न च विशेषो ह्यभावात् (Na Ca Viśeṣo Hyabhāvāt)

Nor is there any distinction, as there is no basis for it.

Na: Not
Ca: And
Viśeṣaḥ: Distinction
Hi: Indeed
Abhāvāt: Because of absence

No valid distinction exists between Brahman and the
individual self, as all differences dissolve in the ultimate reality.

2.1.152 – न च लोकस्यापि विरोधः सम्भवति
(Na Ca Lokasyāpi Virodhaḥ Sambhavati)

Nor is there any contradiction with worldly experience.

Na: Not
Ca: And
Lokasya: Of the world
Api: Even
Virodhaḥ: Contradiction
Sambhavati: Possible

The teachings of Vedanta are not opposed to practical or worldly experience; they explain the deeper reality underlying it.

———————— • ◆ • ————————

2.1.153 – युक्तत्वाच्च प्रमाणम् (Yuktatvācca Pramāṇam)

And it is valid because of its reasonableness.

Yuktatvāt: Reasonableness
Ca: And
Pramāṇam: Validity

The logical coherence of Vedanta strengthens its validity and establishes it as a reliable source of knowledge.

2.1.154 – कृत्स्नस्याभावस्योक्तत्वात् (Kṛtsnasyābhāvasyoktattvāt)

Because the non-existence of all (distinctions) has been stated.

Kṛtsnasya: Of all
Abhāvasya: Non-existence
Uktattvāt: Because it has been stated

The scriptures declare the non-existence of distinctions
in Brahman, affirming its absolute and indivisible nature.

––––––––– · ✦ · –––––––––

2.1.155 – तत्त्वमस्यादिवाक्येभ्यः (Tattvamasyādivākyebhyaḥ)

Because of the sentences like "That Thou Art."

Tattvam: That Thou Art
Asi: You are
Adi: And so on
Vākyebhyaḥ: From sentences

The Mahāvākyas (great sayings) in the Upanishads, such as Tattvamasi
("You are That"), reveal the identity of the individual self with Brahman.
These statements are foundational to Vedanta.

2.1.156 – एकत्वं च श्रुत्यन्तरेभ्यः (Ekatvaṃ Ca Śrutyantarebhyaḥ)

And unity (is known) from other scriptural texts.

Ekatvaṃ: Unity or oneness
Ca: And
Śruti: Vedas
Antarebhyaḥ: From other parts

The unity of the individual self and Brahman is also taught in numerous other Vedic passages, confirming the non-dual nature of reality.

———— · ♦ · ————

2.1.157 – विकल्पात् चाप्रसिद्धम् (Vikalpāt Cāprasiddham)

And because of the impossibility of alternatives.

Vikalpāt: From alternatives
Ca: And
Aprasiddham: Impossibility or lack of proof

Alternative interpretations of the scriptural texts do not hold up under scrutiny, leaving the non-dual interpretation as the only viable understanding.

2.1.158 – प्रकृतिवदवस्थायाम् (Prakṛtivadavasthāyām)

(The individual self) remains as it is, like nature (Prakti).

Prakṛti: Nature or material cause
Vat: Like
Avasthāyām: In the state

Just as Prakṛti retains its essential nature despite undergoing
changes, the self, even when identified with the body and mind,
remains essentially Brahman.

2.1.159 – अनादित्वात् च (Anāditvāt Ca)

And because of its beginninglessness.

Anāditvāt: From being without a beginning
Ca: And

The self and Brahman are eternal and
without origin, reinforcing the doctrine of their essential oneness.

2.1.160 – न च संसारदर्शनात् (Na Ca Saṃsāradarśanāt)

Nor because of the perception of transmigration.

Na: Not
Ca: And
Saṃsāra: Cycle of birth and death
Darśanāt: From perception

The perception of transmigration (rebirth) pertains to ignorance (avidyā) and does not contradict the ultimate oneness of Brahman and the self.

———————— • ◆ • ————————

2.1.161 – दृष्टारं चाज्ञायाम् (Dṛṣṭāraṃ Cājñāyām)

The seer (experiencer) exists only in ignorance.

Dṛṣṭāraṃ: The seer or observer
Ca: And
Ajñāyām: In ignorance

The notion of the self as a limited experiencer arises only under the influence of ignorance and dissolves upon realizing the self's true nature as Brahman.

2.1.162 – स्वाभाव्याच्च न दोषः (Svābhāvyācca Na Doṣaḥ)

And there is no defect because it is its nature.

Svābhāvyāt: Because of its nature
Ca: And
Na: Not
Doṣaḥ: Defect

The apparent duality experienced in the world is a natural outcome of ignorance and does not affect the true non-dual nature of Brahman.

———— · ◆ · ————

2.1.163 – यथाश्रुतं तु (Yathāśrutaṃ Tu)

But as it is taught in the scriptures.

Yathā: As
Śrutam: Heard or taught
Tu: But

The reality of Brahman and its oneness with the self must be understood exactly as it is revealed in the scriptures, without misinterpretation.

2.1.164 – न च ज्ञापकसमर्थ्यम् (Na Ca Jñāpakasamarthyam)

Nor is there any inconsistency in what reveals (knowledge).

Na: Not
Ca: And
Jñāpaka: That which reveals
Samarthyam: Consistency

The scriptures, as a valid means of knowledge, are consistent and capable of revealing the true nature of Brahman without contradiction.

———————— • ◆ • ————————

2.1.165 – प्रतिज्ञाहानिर्वचनान्तरम् (Pratijñāhānirvacanāntaram)

**There is no abandonment of the proposition,
as there is no other explanation.**

Pratijñā: Proposition or assertion
Hāniḥ: Abandonment
Vacanāntaram: Another explanation

The Vedantic proposition of Brahman's oneness cannot be abandoned, as no other explanation satisfactorily resolves the teachings of the scriptures.

2.1.166 – तथा च सान्तरमधिकरणम् (Tathā Ca Sāntaramadhikaraṇam)

And similarly, the substratum with differences.

Tathā: Likewise
Ca: And
Sāntaram: With differences
Adhikaraṇam: Substratum

The substratum (Brahman) accommodates the apparent
differences of the world without itself being affected, just
as a rope remains unchanged even when mistaken for a snake.

———— • ◆ • ————

2.1.167 – न च द्रव्यव्यक्तिव्याप्तिः (Na Ca Dravyavyaktivyāptiḥ)

Nor is there pervasion of substance by individual characteristics.

Na: Not
Ca: And
Dravya: Substance
Vyakti: Individual characteristics
Vyāptiḥ: Pervasion

Individual traits and distinctions do not pervade or affect the
essential nature of Brahman, which remains untouched by diversity.

2.1.168 – न च गुणवच्छब्दः (Na Ca Guṇavacchabdaḥ)

Nor does the word denote qualities.

Na: Not
Ca: And
Guṇa: Qualities
Vat: With
Śabdaḥ: Word

Words like "Brahman" do not imply qualities or attributes
but point to the essential and formless nature of the ultimate reality.

———— · ◆ · ————

2.1.169 – एवं चात्मकत्वोपदेशः (Evaṃ Cātmakatvopadeśaḥ)

Thus is taught the nature of the self.

Evaṃ: Thus
Ca: And
Ātmakatva: Nature of the self
Upadeśaḥ: Teaching

The scriptures consistently teach the self's identity
with Brahman, affirming its infinite and unchanging nature.

2.1.170 – न च प्रत्ययसाम्यं (Na Ca Pratyayasāmyaṃ)

Nor is there uniformity in perception.

Na: Not
Ca: And
Pratyaya: Perception or cognition
Sāmyaṃ: Uniformity

Differences in individual perception arise from ignorance, yet they do not affect the essential unity and non-dual nature of Brahman.

2.1.171 – न च दर्शनान्तरविरोधः (Na Ca Darśanāntaravirodhaḥ)

Nor is there contradiction with other systems of philosophy.

Na: Not
Ca: And
Darśana: Philosophy or viewpoint
Antara: Other
Virodhaḥ: Contradiction

The non-dual interpretation of Vedanta harmonizes with and transcends the partial truths of other philosophical systems, encompassing them in its ultimate vision of unity.

SECTION 2

(SUTRAS 172-216)

2.2.1 (172) – सर्ववेदान्तप्रत्ययाश्च बोध्यप्रत्ययैक्यम्
(Sarvavedāntapratyayāśca Bodhyapratyayaikyam)

**All Vedantic propositions
indicate the unity of the object of knowledge.**

Sarva: All
Vedānta: Vedantic teachings
Pratyayāḥ: Propositions or ideas
Bodhya: That which is to be known
Pratyayaikyam: Unity of knowledge

The teachings of all Vedantic texts consistently affirm the oneness of Brahman, which is the ultimate object of realization.

———— • ◆ • ————

2.2.2 (173) – कारणत्वं तु श्रुतेरेवम् (Kāraṇatvaṃ Tu Śruterevam)

**The causal nature (of Brahman)
is established by the scripture in this way.**

Kāraṇatvaṃ: Causal nature
Tu: But
Śruteḥ: By the scriptures
Evam: Thus

Brahman as the ultimate cause of the universe is repeatedly confirmed through scriptural declarations, emphasizing its role as the origin of all.

2.2.3 (174) – न च दृष्टान्तोपपत्तेः (Na Ca Dṛṣṭāntopapatteḥ)

Nor can it be negated due
to the appropriateness of examples.

Na: Not
Ca: And
Dṛṣṭānta: Example
Upapatteḥ: Appropriateness

The causal nature of Brahman is explained using appropriate examples, such as the spider spinning its web, which align with scriptural assertions and cannot be refuted.

— • ◆ • —

2.2.4 (175) – तदुपत्तेरविशेषात् (Tadupatteraviśeṣāt)

The manifestation of that
(Brahman) is without distinction.

Tad: That
Upatteḥ: Manifestation
Aviśeṣāt: Without distinction

The creation, sustenance, and dissolution of the universe arise from Brahman without differentiation, as Brahman itself is formless and indivisible.

2.2.5 (176) – नास्ति तु तदन्यथा (Nāsti Tu Tadanyathā)

It cannot be otherwise.

Nāsti: Does not exist
Tu: But
Tadanyathā: Otherwise

The existence and functioning of the universe necessarily depend on Brahman, and no alternative explanation suffices.

— · ♦ · —

2.2.6 (177) – दृष्टान्तोपपत्तिरुपम् (Dṛṣṭāntopapattirūpam)

It is in the form of (valid) examples and reasoning.

Dṛṣṭānta: Example
Upapattiḥ: Reasoning
| Rūpam: Form

The Vedantic assertion of Brahman's causality is supported through logical reasoning and analogies, making it comprehensible to the seeker.

2.2.7 (178) – न च प्रत्ययाभावात् (Na Ca Pratyayābhāvāt)

Nor is there a lack of cognition.

Na: Not
Ca: And
Pratyaya: Cognition
Abhāvāt: Absence

The perception of Brahman may not be immediate for all,
but it is revealed through the scriptures and contemplation.

2.2.8 (179) – पूर्वमेव च तथाप्रसिद्धेः (Pūrvameva Ca Tathāprasiddheḥ)

It was already known before, as it was established in this way.

Pūrvam: Before
Eva: Indeed
Ca: And
Tathā: Thus
Prasiddheḥ: Established

The scriptures establish Brahman as the eternal reality,
known through earlier teachings and consistent revelations.

2.2.9 (180) – न च पूर्वकार्यविरोधः (Na Ca Pūrvakāryavirodhaḥ)

Nor is there contradiction with previous effects.

Na: Not
Ca: And
Pūrva: Previous
Kārya: Effects
Virodhaḥ: Contradiction

The nature of Brahman as the cause of the universe does not contradict the empirical experiences of cause and effect in the world.

2.2.10 (181) – अस्यादर्शयित्वाच्च (Asyādarśayitvācca)

And because it is demonstrated through this.

Asya: Of this
Adarśayitvā: Demonstrated
Ca: And

The scriptures and reasoning consistently demonstrate Brahman's nature and its role as the ultimate cause.

2.2.11 (182) – आत्मशब्दात् तु (Āatmaśabdāt Tu)

But (Brahman is established) because of the word "Self."

Ātma: Self
Śabdāt: From the word
Tu: But

The word "Ātman" (Self) used in the scriptures refers to Brahman,
the ultimate reality, indicating its self-existent and eternal nature.

----------- • ♦ • -----------

2.2.12 (183) – तत्र न विकल्प: (Tatra Na Vikalpaḥ)

In that (Brahman), there is no diversity.

Tatra: There
Na: Not
Vikalpaḥ: Diversity

Brahman is non-dual and without any distinctions, as repeatedly affirmed
by Vedantic texts. Any perception of difference arises due to ignorance.

2.2.13 (184) – गुणदोषविभागाभावात् (Guṇadoṣavibhāgābhāvāt)

Because qualities and faults do not apply to it.

Guṇa: Qualities
Doṣa: Faults
Vibhāga: Division
Abhāvāt: Absence

Brahman is beyond all attributes, being free from both merits and defects, as it transcends the realm of duality.

—— • ♦ • ——

2.2.14 (185) – अन्यत्र च परेण शब्दात् (Anyatra Ca Pareṇa Śabdāt)

And elsewhere, by the word indicating the Supreme.

Anyatra: Elsewhere
Ca: And
Pareṇa: Supreme
Śabdāt: From the word

Brahman is referred to as the Supreme Being in various other scriptural contexts, affirming its transcendental nature.

2.2.15 (186) – अन्यथानुपपत्तेः (Anyathānupapatteḥ)

Because otherwise, it cannot be explained.

Anyathā: Otherwise
Anupapatteḥ: Inexplicability

The creation and sustenance of the universe cannot be logically explained without accepting Brahman as the ultimate cause.

———— • ♦ • ————

2.2.16 (187) – कारणत्वाच्च स्थेयः (Kāraṇatvācca Stheyaḥ)

And because of being the cause, it is to be accepted.

Kāraṇatvāt: Due to being the cause
Ca: And
Stheyaḥ: To be accepted

Brahman, being the ultimate cause of the universe, must be accepted as the fundamental principle underlying all existence.

2.2.17 (188) – उपादानग्रहणात् (Upādānagrahaṇāt)

Because of the acceptance of material cause.

Upādāna: Material cause
Grahāṇāt: Acceptance

The scriptures describe Brahman as both the material and efficient cause of the universe, further affirming its non-duality.

2.2.18 (189) – न च शरीरशब्दवत् (Na Ca Śarīraśabdavat)

Nor is it like the term "body."

Na: Not
Ca: And
Śarīra: Body
Śabdavat: Like the term

Brahman is not comparable to material objects or
the body, as it is beyond all physical forms and limitations.

2.2.19 (190) – असंसृतत्वात् (Asaṃsṛtatvāt)

Because it is free from transmigration.

Asaṃsṛtatvāt: Due to being free from transmigration

Brahman is not subject to the cycle of birth and death (samsara) and remains eternally pure and unchanging.

2.2.20 (191) – सत्त्वयोगाच्च (Sattvayogācca)

And because of association with existence.

Sattva: Existence or reality
Yogāt: Due to association
Ca: And

Brahman is described as existence itself in Vedantic texts, reinforcing its fundamental and unchanging nature.

2.2.21 (192) – असम्भवाच्च (Asambhavācca)

And because it is impossible (otherwise).

Asambhavāt: Due to impossibility
Ca: And

The notion of the universe arising without an ultimate cause like Brahman is logically untenable, reinforcing Brahman's necessity as the source of all.

———— · ♦ · ————

2.2.22 (193) – एकत्वात् (Ekatvāt)

Because of its unity.

Ekatvāt: Due to unity

Brahman is singular and non-dual, with no second entity to contradict or compete with its existence, as affirmed by Vedantic teachings.

2.2.23 (194) – व्यपदेशाच्च कार्यकरणयो:
(Vyapadeśācca Kāryakaraṇayoḥ)

And because the instruments and effects are mentioned.

Vyapadeśāt: Due to mention
Kārya: Effect
Karaṇa: Instrument
Yoḥ: Of both

Scriptures describe both the cause (Brahman) and its instruments,
affirming Brahman's integral role in creation and sustenance.

2.2.24 (195) – साक्षाच्चोभयाम्नानात् (Sākṣāccobhayāmnānāt)

And because both (aspects) are directly stated.

Sākṣāt: Directly
Ca: And
Ubhaya: Both
Āmnānāt: From declaration

The scriptures explicitly declare both Brahman's transcendence
and immanence, emphasizing its all-encompassing nature.

2.2.25 (196) – तदन्यत्वे तत्राप्यनन्यत्वम्
(Tadanyatve Tatrāpyananyatvam)

Even if considered different, it is not separate.

Tat: That
Anyatve: In otherness
Tatra: There
Api: Even
Ananyatvam: Non-separateness

Even if one perceives duality, Brahman remains
inseparably connected to all things as their substratum.

———— • ◆ • ————

2.2.26 (197) – उपपन्नं च तन्त्रत्वात् (Upapannaṃ Ca Tantratvāt)

And it is reasonable because it is the foundation.

Upapannaṃ: Reasonable
Ca: And
Tantratvāt: Due to being the foundation

Brahman serves as the logical basis for the existence and
operation of the universe, as affirmed by philosophical reasoning.

2.2.27 (198) – पूर्ववत् (Pūrvavat)

As before.

Pūrvavat: Like before

This sutra reiterates previous conclusions, emphasizing the consistent and eternal nature of Brahman as the cause of the universe.

————————— • ◆ • —————————

2.2.28 (199) – परिणामितं ह्येतत् (Pariṇāmitam Hyetat)

For this is modified.

Pariṇāmitam: Modified
Hi: Indeed
Etat: This

The universe is seen as a transformation or modification of Brahman, affirming Brahman's status as both material and efficient cause.

2.2.29 (200) – दृष्टान्तानुपपत्तेश्च (Dṛṣṭāntānupapatteśca)

And because examples are not applicable otherwise.

Dṛṣṭānta: Example
Anupapatteḥ: Lack of applicability
Ca: And

Scriptural analogies and logical examples consistently point toward Brahman as the ultimate reality, leaving n room for alternative interpretations.

———————— •♦• ————————

2.2.30 (201) – अपि च समित्युक्तेः (Api Ca Samityukteḥ)

And because it is stated in the Vedas.

Api: Also
Ca: And
Samiti: Vedas or scriptures
Ukteḥ: From statement

The Vedas explicitly declare Brahman as the ultimate cause, leaving no ambiguity regarding its central role in creation and sustenance.

2.2.31 (202) – कार्यसामर्थ्यात् (Kāryasāmarthyāt)

Because of the efficiency of the effects.

Kārya: Effect
Sāmarthyāt: Due to efficiency

The orderly and efficient functioning of the universe
implies a single, intelligent cause, identified as Brahman.

2.2.32 (203) – समानचत्वात् (Samānacatvāt)

Because of uniformity.

Samāna: Uniformity or equality
Catvāt: Due to

The universe operates with a remarkable uniformity, which
indicates a single, consistent cause—Brahman—underlying all creation.

2.2.33 (204) – न तत्सामान्यात् (Na Tatsāmānyāt)

Not due to mere similarity.

Na: Not
Tat: That
Sāmānyāt: Due to similarity

The uniformity observed in creation is not because of similarity among entities but because of their origin in Brahman, the singular reality.

2.2.34 (205) – अन्योऽभवस्स्यात् (Anyo'bhavassyāt)

Otherwise, there would be another existence.

Anyaḥ: Another
Abhavaḥ: Existence
Syāt: Would be

If Brahman were not the sole cause, there would be room for a second independent reality, which contradicts the non-dual nature of existence.

2.2.35 (206) – प्रकृतिश्चेन्नोपसंग्रहात् (Prakṛtiścenno'pasaṅgrahāt)

**If it is Prakriti (nature), then also it is
not (valid) because it is not inclusive.**

Prakṛtiḥ: Nature or matter
Cet: If
Na: Not
Upasaṅgrahāt: Not inclusive

If Prakriti (nature) is proposed as the cause of the universe, it fails to account for the conscious and intelligent aspects of creation, unlike Brahman.

———— · ◆ · ————

2.2.36 (207) – न क्रियासंयोगाद्वा (Na Kriyāsaṃyogādvā)

Nor due to mere association with activity.

Na: Not
Kriyā: Action or activity
Saṃyogāt: Association
Vā: Or

The creation of the universe cannot be attributed to
mechanical or unconscious activity alone; it necessitates
an intelligent cause, which is Brahman.

2.2.37 (208) – दृष्टं च (Dṛṣṭam Ca)

And it is seen.

Dṛṣṭam: Seen or observed
Ca: And

Scriptural evidence and direct observation indicate Brahman as the intelligent and purposeful cause of creation.

———— · ◆ · ————

2.2.38 (209) – आत्यन्तिकं च तद्विसेषणं भवेत्
(Ātyantikaṃ Ca Tadviseṣaṇaṃ Bhavet)

And that (cause) would then become absolute.

Ātyantikaṃ: Absolute or ultimate
Ca: And
Tad: That
Viseṣaṇam: Specification
Bhavet: Would be

The cause, Brahman, is absolute and ultimate, beyond all duality and distinctions, as consistently affirmed in Vedanta.

2.2.39 (210) – श्रुतेश्च (Śruteśca)

And because of scriptural authority.

Śruteḥ: From the scriptures
Ca: And

The Vedas and Upanishads repeatedly affirm Brahman as the
ultimate reality and cause of the universe, reinforcing its validity.

———— • ♦ • ————

2.2.40 (211) – कारणत्वाच्चेश्वरस्य नापरम्
(Kāraṇatvāccaiśvarasya Nāparam)

And since God (Ishvara) is the cause, there is nothing else.

Kāraṇatvāt: Due to being the cause
Ca: And
Īśvarasya: Of God or Ishvara
Na: Not
Aparam: Another

Ishvara, identified with Brahman, is the sole cause of
the universe, leaving no room for a secondary or alternative cause.

2.2.41 (212) – न च वेद्यावेदकभावात् (Na Ca Vedyāvedakabhāvāt)

Nor because of the distinction between knower and known.

Na: Not
Ca: And
Vedyā: Of the known
Vedaka: Of the knower
Bhāvāt: Due to the nature

The distinction between the knower and the known is only apparent and arises due to ignorance. In Brahman, there is no such duality.

———— • ♦ • ————

2.2.42 (213) – एकसम्प्रसादात् (Ekasamprasādāt)

Because of the single serene state.

Eka: One, single
Samprasādāt: From serenity or tranquility

The serene and unified state described in the Upanishads refers to the ultimate reality, Brahman, which is singular and free from multiplicity.

2.2.43 (214) – प्रतीयते च तत्कर्मव्यपदेशात्
(Pratīyate Ca Tatkarmavyapadeśāt)

And it is known from the declaration of its actions.

Pratīyate: It is known
Ca: And
Tat: That
Karma: Actions
Vyapadeśāt: From declaration

The Vedas describe Brahman's actions in creating, sustaining, and dissolving the universe, affirming its role as the ultimate cause.

———————— • ♦ • ————————

2.2.44 (215) – श्रुतेः चात्मशब्दात (ŚShruteḥ Cātmaśabdāt)

And from the scriptural use of the word "self."

Śruteḥ: From the scriptures
Ca: And
Ātma: Self
Śabdāt: From the word

The scriptures frequently use the term "Ātman" (Self) to refer to Brahman, indicating its intimate connection with the essence of all beings.

2.2.45 (216) – सर्वविषयत्वाच्च (Sarvaviṣayatvācca)

And because it is the substratum of everything.

Sarva: All
Viṣayatvāt: Substratum or basis
Ca: And

Brahman, as the ultimate reality, serves as the substratum for all objects, actions, and experiences in the universe, as described in Vedantic teachings.

SECTION 3

(SUTRAS 217–269)

2.3.1 (217) – ईक्षत्यधिकारिकं तु बादरायणः सम्भवात्
(Īkṣatyadhikārikaṃ Tu Bādarāyaṇaḥ Sambhavāt)

But the seeing referred to is in regard to the presiding deities, says Bdaryaa, because it is possible.

Īkṣati: Seeing, contemplating
Adhikārikaṃ: Pertaining to the presiding deities
Tu: But
Bādarāyaṇaḥ: Sage Bādarāyaṇa
Sambhavāt: Due to possibility

Explanation: The scripture sometimes describes the contemplation of presiding deities as "seeing." This is reconciled with the idea that Brahman is the ultimate seer, as the deities act under Brahman's direction.

———— • ♦ • ————

2.3.2 (218) – तच्छुतेः (Tacchruteḥ)

Because it is declared by the scriptures.

Tat: That
Śruteḥ: From the scriptures

The scriptures explicitly state that Brahman directs the actions of all beings, including presiding deities, supporting the interpretation of Brahman as the ultimate source of "seeing."

2.3.3 (219) – गौणश्चेन्नात्मशब्दात् (Gauṇaścennaātmaśabdāt)

**If it is said to be metaphorical,
it is not so, because the word "self" is used.**

Gauṇaḥ: Metaphorical
Cet: If
Na: Not
Ātma: Self
Śabdāt: From the word

The reference to Brahman as "self" is not metaphorical but literal,
as it aligns with the core Vedantic teaching that Brahman is the
innermost essence of all beings.

2.3.4 (220) – उपपत्तेश्च (Upapatteśca)

And because it is reasonable.

Upapatteḥ: Logical reasoning
Ca: And

The identification of Brahman as the "self" is logically consistent,
as it serves as the unchanging substratum underlying all change
and diversity in the universe.

2.3.5 (221) – श्रुतोपन्यासाच्च (Śhrutopanyāsācca)

And because it is introduced in the scriptures.

Śruta: From the scriptures
Upanyāsāt: From the introduction
Ca: And

The scriptures repeatedly introduce Brahman as the ultimate
reality and the inner self of all beings, further confirming
its central role in Vedantic teachings.

2.3.6 (222) – अविरोधश्चन्दनवत् (Avirodhaścandanavat)

There is no contradiction, just as in the case of sandalwood.

Avirodhaḥ: No contradiction
Candanavat: Like sandalwood

Just as the fragrance of sandalwood pervades without contradiction, so
does Brahman pervade the universe, harmonizing all apparent dualities.

2.3.7 (223) – सङ्गतिरिति चेद्व्यतिरिक्तः परतः
(Saṅgatiriti Cedvyatiriktaḥ Parataḥ)

**If it is said to be connection (only),
it is not so; it is distinct and supreme.**

Saṅgatiḥ: Connection or relation
Iti: Thus
Cet: If
Vyatiriktaḥ: Distinct
Parataḥ: Supreme

Brahman is not merely a relational entity; it is the supreme and distinct substratum of all existence, transcending mere connections.

———— • ◆ • ————

2.3.8 (224) – उपदेशभेदान्न वा (Upadeśabhedānna Vāa)

Or not, because of difference in teaching.

Upadeśa: Teaching
Bhedāt: Due to difference
Na: Not
Vā: Or

Differences in scriptural descriptions of Brahman are not contradictions but reflect the diverse aspects of Brahman to address varying levels of understanding.

2.3.9 (225) – प्रतीयते च (Pratīyate Ca)

And it is perceived.

Pratīyate: It is perceived
Ca: And

The nature of Brahman as the unchanging substratum is directly perceived through reasoning and experiential insight.

———— • ♦ • ————

2.3.10 (226) – तत्त्वेन चाहिंसाध्याभ्युपगमादविरोधः
(Tattvena Cāhiṃsādhyābhyupagamādavirodhaḥ)

And there is no contradiction because of the acceptance of reality and non-injury as its goal.

Tattvena: In reality
Ca: And
Ahiṃsā: Non-injury
Adhyābhyupagamāt: Due to acceptance
Avirodhaḥ: No contradiction

The teachings of Brahman are aligned with the principles of ultimate reality and ethical conduct like non-violence, ensuring harmony and non-contradiction.

2.3.11 (227) – अन्तरालम्भनं च (Antarālambanaṃ Ca)

And it is supported internally.

Antara: Internal
Ālambanaṃ: Support
Ca: And

The scriptures state that Brahman exists as the inner support of all beings, emphasizing its role as the indwelling reality that sustains everything.

———— ・◆・ ————

2.3.12 (228) – वाक्यशेषात् (Vākyaśeṣāt)

Because of the conclusion of the sentence.

Vākya: Sentence or statement
Śeṣāt: From the conclusion

The concluding parts of scriptural statements consistently point to Brahman as the ultimate reality, ensuring clarity and coherence in interpretation.

2.3.13 (229) – आकाशस्तल्लिङ्गात् (Ākāśastalliṅgāt)

Space (is Brahman) because of the characteristic mark.

Ākāśaḥ: Space
Tat: That
Liṅgāt: From the characteristic mark

Space, as described in certain scriptural contexts, is indicative of Brahman, as it is subtle, pervasive, and the substratum of all elements.

2.3.14 (230) – नानात्मशब्दात् (Nānaātmaśabdāt)

Not so, because of the word "self."

Na: Not
Āna: From
Ātma: Self
Śabdāt: From the word

Space cannot independently be Brahman because the term "self" used in scriptures specifically refers to a conscious, eternal reality—Brahman.

2.3.15 (231) – अन्यत्राभिध्यानात् (Anyatrābhidhyānāt)

Because of the contemplation being elsewhere.

Anyatra: Elsewhere
Abhidhyānāt: From contemplation

Brahman is the object of meditation in contexts where the Upanishads distinguish it from physical or external entities like space.

2.3.16 (232) – नैवमेकेषामस्माच्छब्दात् (Naivamekeṣāmasmācchabdāt)

Not so, for some, because of the use of the word "this."

Na: Not
Evam: Thus
Ekeṣām: For some
Asmāt: From this
Śabdāt: Word

Some scriptural references emphasize "this" to denote Brahman as a tangible, experiential reality, distinct from abstract entities like space.

2.3.17 (233) – आत्मत्वोपगृहीते चान्तः (Ātmatvopagṛhīte Cāntaḥ)

And being accepted as the Self, it is internal.

Ātmatva: Selfhood
Upagṛhīte: Being accepted
Ca: And
Antaḥ: Internal

Brahman, being the Self, is inherently internal and present in all beings as their innermost essence, making it distinct from external elements like space.

———— ·◆· ————

2.3.18 (234) – प्रतिज्ञानामिकं हि प्रकृतं चाक्षुषत्वात्
(Pratijñānāmikam Hi Prakṛtam Cākṣuṣatvāt)

Because the topic is the same and it is perceivable through the senses.

Pratijñānām: Of the propositions
Ikam: One, same
Hi: Indeed
Prakṛtam: The subject matter
Cākṣuṣatvāt: Because of visibility

The continuity of the topic in the Upanishads confirms that Brahman is being referred to, and its effects can be observed indirectly through the senses.

2.3.19 (235) – न भेदात् (Na Bhedāt)

Not so, because of difference.

Na: Not
Bhedāt: Due to difference

Brahman cannot be equated with anything that exhibits division or duality, as it is indivisible and non-dual in nature.

—————— • ♦ • ——————

2.3.20 (236) – दृष्टमिति चेन न सामान्यविशेषात्
(Dṛṣṭamiti Cen Na Sāmānyaviśeṣāt)

If it is said to be seen, it is not so, because of generic and specific characteristics.

Dṛṣṭam: Seen
Iti: Thus
Cet: If
Na: Not
Sāmānya: Generic
Viśeṣāt: Specific

Brahman, being beyond sense perception, cannot be seen. The apparent references to "seeing" relate to specific manifestations, not the unmanifest absolute.

2.3.21 (237) – शास्त्रदृष्ट्या तु उपरमेत्येवमेके
(ŚāShastradṛṣṭyā Tu Uparametyevameke)

But from the scriptural view, cessation takes place; thus, some hold.

Śāstra: Scripture
Dṛṣṭyā: From the view
Tu: But
Uparamet: Ceases
Evam: Thus
Eke: Some

According to some interpretations, the cessation of duality and multiplicity happens when one realizes the oneness of Brahman, as supported by scriptural declarations.

———— • ◆ • ————

2.3.22 (238) – अभावः खभावादिवत् (Abhāvaḥ Khabhāvādivat)

Absence (of multiplicity), like the nature of space.

Abhāvaḥ: Absence
Kha: Space
Bhāvādivat: Like the nature

Just as space is unaffected by the objects within it, Brahman remains unaffected by the appearance of the universe, indicating the absence of intrinsic multiplicity in Brahman.

2.3.23 (239) – स्मृत्यनवकाशदोषप्रसङ्गः (Smṛtyanavakāśadoṣaprasaṅgaḥ)

The defect of contradiction with Smriti texts would arise.

Smṛti: Secondary scriptures
Anavakāśa: Lack of space or contradiction
Doṣa: Defect
Prasaṅgaḥ: Would arise

If Brahman were to be considered divisible or subject to multiplicity, it would contradict secondary scriptures like the Bhagavad Gita, which emphasize Brahman's indivisible nature.

2.3.24 (240) – विप्रतिषेधाच्च (Vipratiṣedhācca)

And because of mutual contradiction.

Vipratiṣedhaḥ: Mutual contradiction
Ca: And

Any theory positing duality or multiplicity in Brahman leads to logical inconsistencies and contradictions with the core Vedantic teaching of non-duality.

2.3.25 (241) – संभाव्यते च (Saṃbhāvyate Ca)

And it is reasonable.

Saṃbhāvyate: It is reasonable
Ca: And

The idea of Brahman as the sole, indivisible reality is reasonable and consistent with both logic and scriptural teachings.

2.3.26 (242) – दृष्टेनैव वाच्यम् (Dṛṣṭenaiva Vācyam)

It must be stated based on what is seen.

Dṛṣṭena: By what is seen
Eva: Indeed
Vācyam: Must be stated

Scriptural statements about Brahman are rooted in observable principles such as causality, which help guide understanding, even though Brahman itself transcends perception.

2.3.27 (243) – प्रतिषेधाच्च न अभावः (Pratiṣedhācca Na Abhāvaḥ)

And there is no non-existence because of negation.

Pratiṣedhāt: From negation
Ca: And
Na: Not
Abhāvaḥ: Non-existence

The negation of attributes in Brahman does not imply non-existence but rather its transcendence beyond material attributes.

———— · ◆ · ————

2.3.28 (244) – एवं च अतः प्राक्च (Evaṃ Ca Ataḥ Prāk Ca)

And thus, it was so even before (creation).

Evaṃ: Thus
Ca: And
Ataḥ: Therefore
Prāk: Before
Ca: And

Brahman existed in its undifferentiated, pure form even before the manifestation of the universe, confirming its eternal and unchanging nature.

2.3.29 (245) – न संभावनायामेव तु ततः प्रमाणाभावः
(Na Saṃbhāvanāyāmeva Tu Tataḥ Pramāṇābhāvaḥ)

**Not merely on the basis of possibility;
rather, there is no valid proof for that.**

Na: Not
Saṃbhāvanāyām: On the basis of possibility
Eva: Only
Tu: But
Tataḥ: Therefore
Pramāṇābhāvaḥ: Absence of valid proof

Speculative possibilities about Brahman's nature without scriptural or logical evidence are insufficient, as Vedanta relies onwell-grounded proof for assertions.

———— · ♦ · ————

2.3.30 (246) – ईक्षणादिभ्यः च अन्तस्तद्व्याप्तेः
(Īkṣaṇādibhyaḥ Ca Antastadvyāpteḥ)

**And because of the vision and
other attributes, it pervades internally.**

Īkṣaṇa: Vision or perception
Ādibhyaḥ: And other (attributes)
Ca: And
Antaḥ: Internally
Tadvyāpteḥ: Because of its pervasiveness

Brahman is described as the source of all creation, and scriptural references to its vision or intention indicate its pervasive and internal presence within all beings.

2.3.31 (247) – विकल्पप्रसङ्गाच्च (Vikalpaprasaṅgācca)

And because alternatives would arise (if Brahman were not one).

Vikalpa: Alternatives
Prasaṅgāt: Would arise
Ca: And

If Brahman were not the singular, undivided reality, numerous contradictions and alternative theories would emerge, disrupting the coherence of Vedantic teachings.

2.3.32 (248) – कल्पनायाम् च प्रत्युक्तम् (Kalpanāyām Ca Pratyuktam)

And in case of (such) imagination, it has already been refuted.

Kalpanāyām: In the case of imagination
Ca: And
Pratyuktam: Already refuted

Any theory suggesting alternative forms or multiple Brahmans has been systematically dismissed in previous discussions through logic and scriptural references.

2.3.33 (249) – अनादित्वाच्च दोषप्रतिषेधः (Anāditvācca Doṣapratiṣedhaḥ)

And because of being beginningless, defects are negated.

Anāditva: Beginninglessness
Ca: And
Doṣa: Defects
Pratiṣedhaḥ: Negation

Brahman, being eternal and without a beginning, cannot be subject to imperfections or limitations associated with created or finite entities.

2.3.34 (250) – उपपत्तेश्चैवम् (Upapatteścaivam)

And thus, it is reasonable.

Upapattiḥ: Reasonableness
Ca: And
Evam: Thus

The eternal, non-dual nature of Brahman aligns with logical reasoning and scriptural declarations, further supporting its validity.

2.3.35 (251) – समन्वयात् च श्रुतेः (Samanvayāt Ca Śruteḥ)

And because of harmony with the scriptures.

Samanvayāt: Harmony
Ca: And
Śruteḥ: Of the scriptures

The teachings of Vedanta, emphasizing the unity and eternality of Brahman, are consistent with scriptural revelations, reinforcing their authenticity.

———————— • ♦ • ————————

2.3.36 (252) – एकेऽपि चात्यन्तनाशं प्रतीयुः
(Eke'pi Cātyantanāśaṃ Pratīyuḥ)

And some assert absolute destruction (of individuality).

Eke: Some
Api: Even
Ca: And
Atyantanāśaṃ: Absolute destruction
Pratīyuḥ: Assert

Certain philosophical schools propose that individuality is entirely dissolved in Brahman upon realization, signifying complete absorption into the non-dual reality.

2.3.37 (253) – नेह नानास्ति किञ्च्यन इतिचेन्न प्रजापतेरिव
(Neha Nānāsti Kiñcana Iticenna Prajāpateriva)

If it is said that there is no diversity here, it is not so, like in the case of
Prajapati.

Na: Not
Iha: Here
Nānā: Diversity
Asti: Exists
Kiñcana: Anything
Prajāpateriva: Like Prajapati

Diversity in appearances arises due to Maya (illusion), yet Brahman remains
unchanged, just as the one Prajapati manifests the many forms of creation
without losing its singularity.

2.3.38 (254) – पर्यायाच्च (Pariyāyācca)

And because of the alternation.

Pariyāyāt: Alternation
Ca: And

The apparent diversity in the world is explained through the alternation of
states or manifestations of the one Brahman, as described in the scriptures.

2.3.39 (255) – विशेषणात् (Viśeṣaṇāt)

Due to the qualifications.

Viśeṣaṇāt: Due to qualifications

The scriptures attribute certain qualifying characteristics to Brahman to make it comprehensible to the human mind, though Brahman itself is beyond all attributes.

————— · ◆ · —————

2.3.40 (256) – भेदव्यपदेशाच्च (Bhedavyapadeśācca)

And because of the declaration of diversity.

Bheda: Diversity
Vyapadeśāt: Declaration
Ca: And

Scriptures occasionally describe the universe in terms of diversity to accommodate human perception, while ultimately teaching the oneness of Brahman.

2.3.41 (257) – तथाहि दर्शयति (Tathāhi Darśayati)

For thus, it (scripture) shows.

Tathā: Thus
Hi: Indeed
Darśayati: Shows

The scriptures point to the unity of Brahman behind
the apparent diversity, as seen in various Upanishadic statements.

———— • ♦ • ————

2.3.42 (258) – विकल्पोपपत्तेश्च (Vikalpopapatteśca)

And because of the reasonableness of alternative explanations.

Vikalpa: Alternatives
Upapatteḥ: Reasonableness
Ca: And

The apparent contradictions in the descriptions of Brahman are resolved
when interpreted as alternative perspectives for understanding its nature.

2.3.43 (259) – स्यात्यन्ताभावेऽपि पारिशेष्यम्
(Syātyantābhāve'pi Pāriśeṣyam)

Even if absolute non-existence is posited, there remains something.

Syāt: Would be
Atyantābhāve: In absolute non-existence
Api: Even
Pāriśeṣyam: Residue

If everything is negated, there must still be something left, which is the unchanging reality of Brahman.

2.3.44 (260) – दृष्टान्तानुपपत्तेश्च (Dṛṣṭāntānupapatteśca)

And because of the unreasonableness of examples.

Dṛṣṭānta: Examples
Anupapatteḥ: Unreasonableness
Ca: And

Examples used to explain Brahman, when taken literally, fail to capture its true essence, highlighting its transcendence beyond human logic.

2.3.45 (261) – अपि च स्मर्यते (Api Ca Smaryate)

And also because it is remembered (in Smriti).

Api: Also
Ca: And
Smaryate: It is remembered

Secondary scriptures (Smriti) support the teachings of
the Upanishads, affirming the non-dual nature of Brahman.

—— • ◆ • ——

2.3.46 (262) – अप्राणो ह्यमनाः शुभ्रः (Aprāṇo Hyamanāḥ Śubhraḥ)

Without vital airs, without mind, pure.

Aprāṇaḥ: Without vital airs
Hi: Indeed
Amanāḥ: Without mind
Śubhraḥ: Pure

Brahman is beyond physiological and psychological
attributes, described as pure and untouched by limitations.

2.3.47 (263) – तथा च शान्ति: (Tathā Ca Śāntiḥ)

And thus, there is peace.

Tathā: Thus
Ca: And
Śāntiḥ: Peace

Realizing the nature of Brahman as pure, unconditioned, and beyond duality leads to ultimate peace and liberation.

2.3.48 (264) – विशेषणाद्विरोध: (Viśeṣaṇādvirodhaḥ)

Conflict arises due to qualifications.

Viśeṣaṇāt: Due to qualifications
Virodhaḥ: Conflict

Any attempt to qualify Brahman leads to contradictions, as it transcends all attributes and dualistic descriptions.

2.3.49 (265) – एवम् च अविरोधः (Evam Ca Avirodhaḥ)

Thus, there is no contradiction.

Evam: Thus
Ca: And
Avirodhaḥ: No contradiction

When understood as attributeless and non-dual, Brahman
aligns perfectly with scriptural and logical consistency.

· ◆ ·

2.3.50 (266) – आत्मकृतत्वात् (ĀAtmakṛtatvāt)

Because it is self-caused.

Ātmakṛtatvāt: Self-caused

Brahman is the ultimate cause, self-existent,
and independent of any external agency.

2.3.51 (267) – दृष्टश्रुतोपदेशात् (Dṛṣṭaśrutopadeśāt)

Because it is seen and taught in the scriptures.

Dṛṣṭa: Seen
Śruta: Heard
Upadeśāt: Taught

The nature of Brahman as the ultimate reality is supported by both direct experience (as in mystical insights) and scriptural teachings, providing a holistic understanding.

———— • ♦ • ————

2.3.52 (268) – आत्मनः पूर्वत्वात् (Ātmanaḥ Pūrvatvāt)

Because of the prior existence of the Self.

Ātmanaḥ: Of the Self
Pūrvatvāt: Due to being prior

Brahman, as the Self, is eternal and existed before all creation, reinforcing its status as the foundational reality of the universe.

2.3.53 (269) – न ह्यतः पूर्वमपरं वा (Na Hyataḥ Pūrvamaparaṃ Vā)

Neither before this nor after this
(does anything exist independently).

Na: Not
Hi: Indeed
Ataḥ: From this (Brahman)
Pūrvam: Before
Aparam: After
Vā: Or

Nothing exists independently of Brahman, either prior to or subsequent to creation, affirming Brahman's timeless and all-encompassing nature.

SECTION 4

(SUTRAS 270–291)

2.4.1 (270) – अस्मिन्सम्बन्धेऽभिधानाच्च
(Asmin Sambandhe'bhidhānācca)

Because of the declaration of this relationship.

Asmin: In this
Sambandhe: Relationship
Abhidhānāt: Declaration
Ca: And

The scriptures declare the relationship between the individual self (Jiva) and Brahman, emphasizing their unity despite apparent distinctions.

—————— •♦• ——————

2.4.2 (271) – आकाशस्रष्टृत्वादिनिर्देशात् (Ākāśasraṣṭṛtvādinirdeśāt)

Because of the description of the creation of space and so on.

Ākāśa: Space
Sraṣṭṛtva: Creation
Ādi: And so on
Nirdeśāt: Description

Brahman is described as the creator of space, time, and the universe, indicating its supremacy and role as the ultimate reality.

2.4.3 (272) – न वायुकर्मविभागादिति चेत् न स्वाभाव्याद्धर्मवत्
(Na Vāyukarmavibhāgāditi Chet Na Svābhāvyāddharmavat)

**If it is argued that it is due to the division of air
and actions, it is not so, as it is inherent like virtues.**

Na: Not
Vāyu: Air
Karma: Action
Vibhāgāt: Division
Iti Chet: If it is argued
Svābhāvyāt: Due to inherent nature
Dharmavat: Like virtues

The diversity in creation cannot be solely attributed to the division of natural elements and actions. It is inherently rooted in Brahman, just as virtues are intrinsic to individuals.

2.4.4 (273) – कर्मफलाधिकरणं तु एवमेव
(Karmaphalādhikaraṇaṃ Tu Evameva)

But the dispensation of the fruits of action is exactly like this.

Karma: Action
Phala: Fruit
Ādhikaraṇam: Dispensation
Tu: But
Evam: Thus
Eva: Exactly

The administration of the results of actions is explained as being governed by Brahman's inherent law and not arbitrary processes.

2.4.5 (274) – ईश्वरस्य च सम्यग्रूपवत्वात्
(ĪśIsvarasya Ca Samyagrūpavatvāt)

And because the Lord is of a perfect nature.

Īsvarasya: Of the Lord
Ca: And
Samyagrūpavatvāt: Due to being of a perfect nature

Brahman, as the Lord, possesses a flawless and complete nature, making it capable of governing the universe effectively and impartially.

--- • ---

2.4.6 (275) – प्रमाणतश्च तथाहि (Pramāṇataśca Tathāhi)

And indeed, this is so based on valid means of knowledge.

Pramāṇataḥ: Based on valid knowledge
Ca: And
Tathā: Thus
Hi: Indeed

The unity and supremacy of Brahman are established through valid means of knowledge such as perception, inference, and scriptural testimony.

2.4.7 (276) – आनन्दमयोऽभ्यासात् (Ānandamayo'bhyāsāt)

(Brahman is) full of bliss, as repeatedly stated in scriptures.

Ānandamayaḥ: Full of bliss
Abhyāsāt: Due to repeated assertion

Brahman is described as being inherently blissful,
as reiterated in various Upanishadic texts to emphasize its nature.

2.4.8 (277) – उपपत्तेश्च (Upapatteśca)

And because it is reasonable.

Upapatteḥ: Reasonableness
Ca: And

The notion of Brahman being blissful aligns with logic,
as it is the ultimate cause of all joy and fulfillment.

2.4.9 (278) – विपर्ययोऽधिष्ठानात् (Viparyayo'dhiṣṭhānāt)

The opposite (of Brahman) is based on illusion.

Viparyayaḥ: Opposite
Adhiṣṭhānāt: Based on illusion

Misunderstanding or perceiving Brahman as limited or impure arises due to ignorance and illusion, not the true nature of Brahman.

2.4.10 (279) – भवत्येवम् च (Bhavatyevam Ca)

And thus, it indeed happens.

Bhavati: Happens
Evam: Thus
Ca: And

The scriptures confirm that upon the realization of Brahman's blissful nature, ignorance and its effects are dispelled.

2.4.11 (280) – आभासवत् उपलब्धेः (Ābhāsavat Upalabdheḥ)

As with a reflection, due to perception.

Ābhāsavat: Like a reflection
Upalabdheḥ: Due to perception

Just as a reflection suggests the presence of a real object, the perception of joy in the world indicates the existence of the blissful Brahman.

———— • ♦ • ————

2.4.12 (281) – स्मृतेश्च (Smṛteśca)

And also because of Smriti.

Smṛteḥ: Due to Smriti (secondary scriptures)
Ca: And

Secondary scriptures like the Bhagavad Gita affirm the nature of Brahman as the ultimate bliss, complementing primary Upanishadic texts.

2.4.13 (282) – यथाच शरत्प्रज्ञावदुपदेशः
(Yathāca Śaratprajnāvadupadeśaḥ)

As in the case of the instruction of Shataprajn (a sage).

Yathā: As
Ca: And
Śaratprajnāvat: Like Shataprajnā
Upadeśaḥ: Instruction

The teachings and realizations of sages like Shataprajnā serve
as further testimony to the blissful and infinite nature of Brahman.

———— • ◆ • ————

2.4.14 (283) – तदपि न केवलं अविशेषात् (Tadapi Na Kevalam Aviśeṣāt)

Even that is not exclusive, because it is not distinct.

Tadapi: Even that
Na: Not
Kevalam: Exclusive
Aviśeṣāt: Due to non-distinction

While individual experiences of bliss may seem unique, they are
fundamentally rooted in the undivided nature of Brahman.

2.4.15 (284) – प्रजापतेर्व्याचष्टे: (Prajāpatervyācaṣṭeḥ)

Because of the explanation by Prajapati (the creator).

Prajāpateḥ: Of Prajapati
Vyācaṣṭeḥ: Explanation

Prajapati's teachings in the Upanishads emphasize
Brahman's blissful essence and its role as the ultimate goal of life.

2.4.16 (285) – किं पुनरुपलब्धे: (Kiṃ Punarupalabdheḥ)

Why again? Because of realization.

Kiṃ: Why
Punaḥ: Again
Upalabdheḥ: Realization

Realization of Brahman's blissful nature removes all doubts,
confirming its ultimate reality beyond theoretical understanding.

2.4.17 (286) – प्रमाणेऽपि च दर्शयति (Pramāṇe'pi Ca Darśayati)

And it is also shown in valid sources of knowledge.

Pramāṇe: In valid knowledge
Api: Also
Ca: And
Darśayati: Shows

Scriptures, along with reasoning and personal experiences, affirm the blissful and infinite nature of Brahman.

———— • ♦ • ————

2.4.18 (287) – यतश्चेत्तस्य तद्व्यपदेशः (Yataścettasya Tadvyapadeśaḥ)

If it were so, then it is described as such.

Yataḥ: If
Cet: So
Tasya: Of it
Tadvyapadeśaḥ: Such description

If Brahman were finite or lacking, the scriptures would not describe it as infinite bliss, proving its transcendental nature.

2.4.19 (288) – तत्तद्वचनाच्च (Tattadvacanācca)

And because of such statements (in scriptures).

Tattat: Such
Vacanāt: Statements
Ca: And

The consistent declarations in various scriptures regarding
Brahman's blissful and infinite nature further establish its ultimate reality.

— ◆ —

2.4.20 (289) – न ह्येतस्मिन्प्रवर्तकः श्रुतिः प्रमाणम्
(Na Hyetaminpravartakaḥ Śrutiḥ Pramāṇam)

The scriptures are not authoritative in this matter.

Na: Not
Hi: Indeed
Etasmin: In this
Pravartakaḥ: Authoritative
Śrutiḥ: Scriptures
Pramāṇam: Valid knowledge

When it comes to direct experience of Brahman, scriptures
are secondary; realization and self-evidence take precedence.

2.4.21 (290) – ब्रह्मणः प्रमाणं च ततः स्मृतिः
(Brahmaṇaḥ Pramāṇam Ca Tataḥ Smṛtiḥ)

Brahman's nature is proven by scripture and Smriti.

Brahmaṇaḥ: Of Brahman
Pramāṇam: Proof
Ca: And
Tataḥ: Therefore
Smṛtiḥ: Secondary scriptures

Both primary scriptures (Shruti) and secondary scriptures (Smriti) provide consistent evidence for the nature of Brahman as the ultimate bliss.

2.4.22 (291) – अतोऽनन्तं तत्सिद्धम् (Ato'nantaṃ Tatsiddham)

Therefore, it is infinite, as established.

Ataḥ: Therefore
Anantam: Infinite
Tatsiddham: Established

Brahman's infinite and blissful nature is firmly established through scriptures, reasoning, and personal realization.

CHAPTER 3

SECTION 1

(SUTRAS 292-318)

3.1.1 (292) – तथा प्रसक्तं हि विशेषणम् (Tathā Prasaktaṃ Hi Viśeṣaṇam)

Thus, the qualification is indeed appropriate.

Tathā: Thus
Prasaktam: Appropriate
Hi: Indeed
Viśeṣaṇam: Qualification

Explanation: The specific attributes or qualities ascribed to
Brahman in scriptures are fitting and serve the purpose
of distinguishing it from other entities.

3.1.2 (293) – दर्शनाच्च (Darśanācca)

And because of the scriptural declaration.

Darśanāt: From the declaration
Ca: And

The scriptures explicitly declare the attributes of
Brahman, further affirming its supreme and unique nature.

3.1.3 (294) – उपदेशभेदान्नित्यत्वमभ्युपगच्छन्ति हि
(Upadeśabhedānnityatvamabhyupagacchanti Hi)

**Because of the difference in teaching,
(the scriptures) accept its eternality.**

Upadeśa: Teaching
Bhedāt: Difference
Nityatvam: Eternity
Abhyupagacchanti: Accept
Hi: Indeed

The eternal nature of Brahman is taught differently in various contexts, but all affirm its changeless and everlasting essence.

————— • ◆ • —————

3.1.4 (295) – तेन ह्यन्तवद्विशेषणम् (Tena Hyantavadviśeṣaṇam)

Hence, the qualification is not finite.

Tena: Hence
Hi: Indeed
Antavat: Finite
Viśeṣaṇam: Qualification

Any attribute of Brahman described in scriptures does not imply limitation but is a means to understand its infinite nature.

3.1.5 (296) – हेतुचोदनायां तु (Hetucodanāyāṃ Tu)

But in prescribing a cause.

Hetu: Cause
Codanāyām: Prescription
Tu: But

When scriptures attribute causality to Brahman, it is to explain the creation, preservation, and dissolution of the universe, not to limit its nature.

———— • ♦ • ————

3.1.6 (297) – एतेन समाख्यानं व्याख्यातम् (Etena Samākhyānaṃ Vyākhyātam)

By this, the name is explained.

Etena: By this
Samākhyānam: Name
Vyākhyātam: Explained

The names and titles ascribed to Brahman in the scriptures are explained through its attributes and activities.

3.1.7 (298) – तदनुग्रहमेव चेष्टनम् (Tadanugrahameva Ceṣṭanam)

And its activity is indeed for grace.

Tadanugraham: Its grace
Eva: Indeed
Ceṣṭanam: Activity

Brahman's actions, as described in creation and guidance,
are aimed at benefiting the individual self through its grace.

• ◆ •

3.1.8 (299) – लोकवत्तु लीलाकैवल्यम् (Lokavattu Līlākaivalyam)

But like the world, it is purely a play.

Lokavat: Like the world
Tu: But
Līlā: Play
Kaivalyam: Absolute freedom

Brahman's involvement in creation is not out of necessity but out of
its inherent freedom and as a playful expression of its blissful nature.

3.1.9 (300) – शङ्केः वैतथ्यं वचनात् (Śaṅkeḥḥ Vaitathyaṃ Vacanāt)

The doubt is unfounded, as stated in the scriptures.

Śaṅkeḥ: Of doubt
Vaitathyam: Unfounded
Vacanāt: From the statement

Any doubts regarding Brahman's nature are resolved
through clear scriptural declarations of its reality and supremacy.

———————— • ◆ • ————————

3.1.10 (301) – स्मर्यते च अन्यथा (Smaryate Ca Anyathā)

And it is also remembered otherwise.

Smaryate: Remembered
Ca: And
Anyathā: Otherwise

Brahman is also remembered in diverse ways in the scriptures,
reflecting its multifaceted manifestations in the universe.

3.1.11 (302) – एवं चाऽत्र शिष्टपरिग्रहः (Evaṃ Cā'tra Śiṣṭaparigraḥ)

Thus, in this case, the acceptance of the wise.

Evaṃ: Thus
Ca: And
Atra: Here
Śiṣṭa: Wise
Parigrahaḥ: Acceptance

The understanding of Brahman as described in the scriptures aligns with the wisdom and acceptance of enlightened sages.

———— • ◆ • ————

3.1.12 (303) – अप्रसिद्धेश्च (Aprasiddheśca)

And because of unfamiliarity.

Aprasiddheḥ: Unfamiliarity
Ca: And

Brahman is not easily grasped by the unenlightened due to its subtle and transcendental nature.

3.1.13 (304) – एतेन सर्वत्र प्रत्यवसानं दृष्टम्
(Etena Sarvatra Pratyavasānaṃ Dṛṣṭam)

By this, the culmination everywhere is observed.

Etena: By this
Sarvatra: Everywhere
Pratyavasānam: Culmination
Dṛṣṭam: Observed

All scriptural declarations culminate in the
realization of Brahman as the ultimate truth and goal.

———— • ◆ • ————

3.1.14 (305) – तथा हि दर्शयति (Tathā Hi Darśayati)

Thus, indeed, it is shown.

Tathā: Thus
Hi: Indeed
Darśayati: Shows

The scriptures explicitly point to Brahman as the
supreme reality and the foundation of all existence.

3.1.15 (306) – सामान्याच्च यथा लौकिकः (Sāmānyācca Yathā Laukikaḥ)

And because of the generality, like in the worldly.

Sāmānyāt: Due to generality
Ca: And
Yathā: As
Laukikaḥ: Worldly

The relationship between the individual soul and Brahman can be understood through analogies in the worldly experience, aiding comprehension.

3.1.16 (307) – विशिष्टफलेऽप्युपपत्तेः (Viśiṣṭaphale'pyupapatteḥ)

Even when the result is specific, it is appropriate.

Viśiṣṭaphale: Specific result
Api: Even
Upapatteḥ: Appropriateness

Even in cases where Brahman is associated with particular results, its transcendental and infinite nature remains unaffected.

3.1.17 (308) – अथ यज्ञादिवत् (Atha Yajñādivat)

As in the case of sacrifices and the like.

Atha: As
Yajñādivat: Like sacrifices

Just as sacrifices have specific rituals and outcomes, the realization of Brahman involves specific practices and results, guided by the scriptures.

———— • ◆ • ————

3.1.18 (309) – आत्मनः कर्तृत्वादिवदिति चेत्
(Ātmanaḥ Kartṛtvādivaditi Cet)

If it is argued, like the agency of the self.

Ātmanaḥ: Of the self
Kartṛtvād: Agency
Iti: Thus
Cet: If

It may be contended that the soul's actions resemble Brahman's agency, but Brahman is beyond all action and duality.

3.1.19 (310) – न धृत्यादिवत् (Na Dhṛtyādivat)

Not like firmness and the like.

Na: Not
Dhṛtyādi: Firmness and similar qualities
Vat: Like

The attributes ascribed to Brahman, such as firmness,
are not limiting but point to its transcendent nature.

3.1.20 (311) – तस्मिन्नसम्भवात् (Tasminn Asambhavāt)

Because it is impossible in that (Brahman).

Tasmin: In that
Asambhavāt: Due to impossibility

Actions, duality, or qualities attributed to Brahman
are ultimately impossible as it is beyond all distinctions.

3.1.21 (312) – आनन्दमयत्वादेव च (Ānandamayatvādeva Ca)

And because of its nature as pure bliss.

Ānandamaya: Blissful |
Tvāt: Due to
| Eva: Indeed
Ca: And

Brahman is described as Ānandamaya (full of bliss),
which confirms its infinite and non-dual nature.

3.1.22 (313) – विशेषाच्च शास्त्रदर्शनात् (Viśeṣācca Śāstradarśanāt)

And because of distinctions mentioned in the scriptures.

Viśeṣāt: Due to distinctions
Ca: And
Śāstradarśanāt: From scriptural reference

The scriptures describe Brahman as distinct from
the universe, confirming its supreme transcendence.

3.1.23 (314) – अन्यत्रोपपत्ते: (Anyatropapatteḥ)

Because it is possible elsewhere.

Anyatra: Elsewhere
Upapatteḥ: Because of possibility

Brahman's attributes are uniquely applicable to it and not to other entities, which supports its distinction and transcendence.

3.1.24 (315) – प्रसक्तं तु कर्म फलात् (Prasaktaṃ Tu Karma Phalāt)

But actions are connected with results.

Prasaktam: Connected
Tu: But
Karma: Actions
Phalāt: Results

Actions performed by individuals in the material world inevitably lead to results. However, Brahman remains beyond these causal connections, being untouched by actions or outcomes.

3.1.25 (316) – नैवमसङ्गस्य तद्वचनात् (Naivamasaṅgasya Tadvacanāt)

Not so for the unattached, as declared in scriptures.

Na: Not
Evam: Thus
Asaṅgasya: Of the unattached
Tadvacanāt: As declared

Brahman, being unattached and independent,
is not bound by the laws of karma, as clearly stated in the scriptures.
Its nature is ever-free and beyond the limitations of action and results.

———— • ◆ • ————

3.1.26 (317) – स्मरन्ति च (Smaranti Ca)

And (this) is remembered (in the Smritis).

Smaranti: Remembered
Ca: And

The Smritis (secondary scriptures) also affirm that Brahman
is beyond attachment, action, and the outcomes of karma,
emphasizing its transcendental and unaffected state.

3.1.27 (318) – तदुक्तं च प्रत्ययशब्दात् (Taduktaṃ Ca Pratyayaśabdāt)

That has been said (in scriptures) because of words indicating faith.

Tad: That
Uktam: Has been said
Ca: And
Pratyayaśabdāt: Words indicating faith

The scriptures assert that faith and knowledge lead to the realization of Brahman, which is free from karma and the cycle of cause and effect. Brahman is revealed through these scriptural affirmations, guiding seekers towards liberation.

SECTION 2

(SUTRAS 319-359)

3.2.1 (319) – न कर्माविभागादिति चेत् नानाधिकरण्यमनपेक्षा
(Na Karmāvibhāgāditi Chet Nā'nādhikaraṇyam Anapekṣā)

**If it is argued that there is no distinction due to action,
it is not so, as they pertain to different contexts and purposes.**

Na: Not
Karmāvibhāgāt: Due to lack of distinction in action
Anādhikaraṇyam: Different context
Anapekṣā: Without dependency

The results of actions and the qualifications for specific rites are
distinct due to the differing contexts and intentions of individuals.

3.2.2 (320) – न वा परात्मशब्दात् (Na Vā Parātmaśabdāt)

Or rather, not so, due to the usage of the term "Supreme Self."

Na: Not
Vā: Or rather
Parātmaśabdāt: Due to the term "Supreme Self"

The term "Supreme Self" in the scriptures refers to Brahman,
which transcends any association with specific actions or rituals.

3.2.3 (321) – आश्रमकर्माऽपि हि गृह्यते तत्करणात्
(Āśramakarmāpi Hi Gṛhyate Tatkaraṇāt)

The duties of the different stages of life are accepted, as they serve specific purposes.

Āśramakarma: Duties of different life stages
Hi: Indeed
Gṛhyate: Accepted
Tatkaraṇāt: Due to their purpose

The prescribed duties of life stages, like studenthood or householder life, are upheld as they are instrumental for spiritual progress.

———————— •◆• ————————

3.2.4 (322) – सविज्ञानम् एवम् (Savijñānam Evam)

Thus, knowledge is accompanied by realization.

Savijñānam: With realization
Evam: Thus

Mere intellectual understanding of the scriptures is insufficient; one must realize the truths experientially for liberation.

3.2.5 (323) – स्वाभाव्यान्यत्वम् (Svābhāvyānyatvam)

The distinction arises from the inherent nature.

Svābhāvya: Inherent nature
Anyatvam: Distinction

Differences in the results of actions and duties stem from
the inherent characteristics and nature of individuals.

3.2.6 (324) – प्रधानव्यपदेशः सूत्रार्थवत्त्वात् (Pradhānavyapadeśaḥ Sūtrārthavattvāt)

The mention of Pradhāna (non-Brahman entity)
serves to clarify the meaning of the sutra.

Pradhāna: Non-Brahman entity
Vyapadeśaḥ: Mention
Sūtrārthavattvāt: To clarify the sutra's meaning

The mention of Pradhāna in certain texts clarifies its role
as subordinate to Brahman and not independent in creation.

3.2.7 (325) – दार्शनिकम् इव दृश्यते (Dārśanikam Iva Dṛśyate)

It appears as though it is based on philosophical reasoning.

Dārśanikam: Philosophical
Iva: As though
Dṛśyate: Appears

Certain scriptural assertions seem philosophical in nature,
yet they ultimately point to Brahman as the highest reality.

3.2.8 (326) – तत्रापि तद्व्यक्तिरविरोधः (Tatrāpi Tadvyaktir Avidodhaḥ)

Even there, its manifestation is not contradicted.

Tatra: There
Api: Even
Tadvyaktiḥ: Its manifestation
Avidodhaḥ: Not contradicted

The manifestation of Brahman is consistent and
free from contradiction in all scriptural contexts.

3.2.9 (327) – साङ्ख्योपपत्तेः अन्यथा (Sāṅkhyopapatteḥ Anyathā)

Otherwise, it contradicts the Sankhya philosophy.

Sāṅkhya: Sankhya philosophy
Upapatteḥ: Logical explanation
Anyathā: Otherwise

Rejecting Brahman's supremacy would contradict logical principles upheld by Sankhya and other philosophical systems.

———— • ◆ • ————

3.2.10 (328) – तदयोगादेव ततः आचिन्त्यत्वम्
(Tadayogādeva Tataḥ Ācintyatvam)

Due to its inapplicability, it is considered inconceivable.

Tadayogāt: Inapplicability
Eva: Indeed
Tataḥ: Therefore
Ācintyatvam: Inconceivability

Brahman transcends human thought and logic; hence,
it is described as beyond the grasp of ordinary reasoning.

3.2.1 (319) – न कर्माविभागादिति चेत् नानाधिकरण्यमनपेक्षा
(Na Karmāvibhāgāditi Chet Nā'nādhikaraṇyam Anapekṣā)

If it is argued that there is no distinction due to action,
it is not so, as they pertain to different contexts and purposes.

Na: Not
Karmāvibhāgāt: Due to lack of distinction in action
Anādhikaraṇyam: Different context
Anapekṣā: Without dependency

The results of actions and the qualifications for specific rites are
distinct due to the differing contexts and intentions of individuals.

— • ◆ • —

3.2.2 (320) – न वा परात्मशब्दात् (Na Vā Parātmaśabdāt)

Or rather, not so, due to the usage of the term "Supreme Self."

Na: Not
Vā: Or rather
Parātmaśabdāt: Due to the term "Supreme Self"

The term "Supreme Self" in the scriptures refers to Brahman,
which transcends any association with specific actions or rituals.

3.2.3 (321) – आश्रमकर्मापि हि गृह्यते तत्करणात्
(Āśramakarmāpi Hi Gṛhyate Tatkaraṇāt)

**The duties of the different stages of life
are accepted, as they serve specific purposes.**

Āśramakarma: Duties of different life stages
Hi: Indeed
Gṛhyate: Accepted
Tatkaraṇāt: Due to their purpose

The prescribed duties of life stages, like studenthood or householder life, are upheld as they are instrumental for spiritual progress.

————— • ♦ • —————

3.2.4 (322) – सविज्ञानम् एवम् (Savijñānam Evam)

Thus, knowledge is accompanied by realization.

Savijñānam: With realization
Evam: Thus

Mere intellectual understanding of the scriptures is insufficient; one must realize the truths experientially for liberation.

3.2.5 (323) – स्वाभाव्यान्यत्वम् (Svābhāvyānyatvam)

The distinction arises from the inherent nature.

Svābhāvya: Inherent nature
Anyatvam: Distinction

Differences in the results of actions and duties stem from the inherent characteristics and nature of individuals.

3.2.6 (324) – प्रधानव्यपदेशः सूत्रार्थवत्त्वात्
(Pradhānavyapadeśaḥ Sūtrārthavattvāt)

The mention of Pradhna (non-Brahman entity) serves to clarify the meaning of the sutra.

Pradhāna: Non-Brahman entity
Vyapadeśaḥ: Mention
Sūtrārthavattvāt: To clarify the sutra's meaning

The mention of Pradhāna in certain texts clarifies its role as subordinate to Brahman and not independent in creation.

3.2.7 (325) – दार्शनिकम् इव दृश्यते (Dārśanikam Iva Dṛśyate)

It appears as though it is based on philosophical reasoning.

Dārśanikam: Philosophical
Iva: As though
Dṛśyate: Appears

Certain scriptural assertions seem philosophical in nature,
yet they ultimately point to Brahman as the highest reality.

3.2.8 (326) – तत्रापि तद्व्यक्तिरविरोधः (Tatrāpi Tadvyaktir Avidodhaḥ)

Even there, its manifestation is not contradicted.

Tatra: There
Api: Even
Tadvyaktiḥ: Its manifestation
Avidodhaḥ: Not contradicted

The manifestation of Brahman is consistent and
free from contradiction in all scriptural contexts.

3.2.9 (327) – साङ्ख्योपपत्तेः अन्यथा (Sāṅkhyopapatteḥ Anyathā)

Otherwise, it contradicts the Sankhya philosophy.

Sāṅkhya: Sankhya philosophy
Upapatteḥ: Logical explanation
Anyathā: Otherwise

Rejecting Brahman's supremacy would contradict logical principles upheld by Sankhya and other philosophical systems.

3.2.10 (328) – तदयोगादेव ततः आचिन्त्यत्वम्
(Tadayogādeva Tataḥ Ācintyatvam)

Due to its inapplicability, it is considered inconceivable.

Tadayogāt: Inapplicability
Eva: Indeed
Tataḥ: Therefore
Ācintyatvam: Inconceivability

Brahman transcends human thought and logic; hence,
it is described as beyond the grasp of ordinary reasoning.

3.2.10 (328) – तदयोगादेव ततः आचिन्त्यत्वम्
(Tadayogādeva Tataḥ Ācintyatvam)

Due to its inapplicability, it is considered inconceivable.

Tadayogāt: Inapplicability
Eva: Indeed
Tataḥ: Therefore
Ācintyatvam: Inconceivability

Brahman transcends human thought and logic; hence,
it is described as beyond the grasp of ordinary reasoning.

—— · ◆ · ——

3.2.11 (329) – शास्त्रार्थवत्त्वं च तत्सिद्धेः
(Śāstrārthavattvaṁ Ca Tatsiddheḥ)

The scripture's meaningfulness is established by realizing that.

Śāstrārthavattvam: Meaningfulness of scripture
Ca: And
Tatsiddheḥ: Its realization

The authority and intent of the scriptures are
fulfilled when the true nature of Brahman is realized.

3.2.12 (330) – अपूर्वत्वं च ब्रह्मशब्दात् (Apūrvatvaṁ Ca Brahmaśabdāt)

Uniqueness (of Brahman) is derived from the term "Brahman."

Apūrvatvam: Uniqueness
Ca: And
Brahmaśabdāt: From the term "Brahman"

Brahman is unique and unparalleled, as the term
itself signifies infinite existence, knowledge, and bliss.

———————— • ◆ • ————————

3.2.13 (331) – अन्यत्वानुपपत्तेश्च (Anyatvānupapatteśca)

Because the assumption of anything other than Brahman is unreasonable.

Anyatva: Otherness
Anupapatteḥ: Unreasonableness
Ca: And

Brahman is all-encompassing; hence, the existence
of anything truly distinct or separate from it is illogical.

3.2.14 (332) – तद्व्यपदेशाच्च (Tadvyapadeśācca)

Because it is so declared.

Tadvyapadeśāt: From such declaration
Ca: And

The scriptures consistently declare that Brahman alone
is the ultimate reality, eliminating the possibility of duality.

————————— · ♦ · —————————

3.2.15 (333) – परिणामशब्दाच्च (Pariṇāmaśabdācca)

And because of the use of the term "transformation."

Pariṇāma: Transformation
Śabdāt: From the term
Ca: And

The scriptures describe the world as a transformation
of Brahman, emphasizing its unity with the ultimate cause.

3.2.16 (334) – अपि च स्मर्यते (Api Ca Smaryate)

And this is also remembered (in Smriti).

Api: Also
Ca: And
Smaryate: Remembered

Both Smriti and Shruti affirm that Brahman is the substratum
of all existence, strengthening the argument for its unity.

— • ◆ • —

3.2.17 (335) – चोदनादिभ्यः (Codanādibhyaḥ)

From the scriptural injunctions and other statements.

Codanā: Scriptural injunctions
Ādibhyaḥ: And others

The teachings of the scriptures direct individuals toward
the understanding of Brahman as the one ultimate reality.

3.2.18 (336) – अन्यथानुपपत्तेश्च (Anyathānupapatteśca)

And because of the impossibility of any other explanation.

Anyathā: Otherwise
Anupapatteḥ: Impossibility
Ca: And

Any interpretation that denies Brahman as the ultimate reality
fails to account for the scriptural teachings and the nature of existence.

3.2.19 (337) – कारणत्वं च (Kāraṇatvaṁ Ca)

And because of causality.

Kāraṇatvam: Causality
Ca: And

Brahman is the ultimate cause of the universe, as affirmed
by the scriptures, highlighting its unique position as the source of all.

3.2.20 (338) – कार्यं च परिणामात् (Kāryaṁ Ca Pariṇāmāt)

The effect (world) arises from transformation.

Kāryaṁ: Effect
Ca: And
Pariṇāmāt: From transformation

The world, as the effect, is a transformation of Brahman, demonstrating its causal relationship with creation.

— • ◆ • —

3.2.21 (339) – उपपत्तेश्च (Upapatteśca)

And because it is reasonable.

Upapatteḥ: Reasonableness
Ca: And

The idea that Brahman is both the material and efficient cause of the universe aligns with logical reasoning and scriptural authority.

3.2.22 (340) – ब्रह्मकृतिः च श्रुतेः (Brahmakṛtiḥ Ca Śruteḥ)

The creation is of Brahman, as revealed by the scriptures.

Brahmakṛtiḥ: Creation of Brahman
Ca: And
Śruteḥ: From the scriptures

The scriptures explicitly declare that Brahman is the source
of all creation, reinforcing its position as the ultimate cause.

3.2.23 (341) – तस्माच्च कारणत्वं (Tasmācca Kāraṇatvaṁ)

Therefore, causality belongs to Brahman.

Tasmāt: Therefore
Ca: And
Kāraṇatvaṁ: Causality

Brahman's nature as the cause of the universe is firmly
established by both logical reasoning and scriptural declarations.

3.2.24 (342) – सत्त्वसञ्ज्ञमन्तरभवति चादृश्यम्
(Sattvasañjñam Antarabhavati Cādṛśyam)

Within creation arises the quality of existence, which is imperceptible.

Sattvasañjñam: Quality of existence
Antara: Within
Bhavati: Arises
Ca: And
Adṛśyam: Imperceptible

In the process of creation, existence manifests in subtle, imperceptible forms before becoming apparent.

—— • ◆ • ——

3.2.25 (343) – असम्भवाच्य निरवयवत्वात्
(Asambhavācca Niravayayavatvāt)

And because Brahman is partless, division is impossible.

Asambhavāt: Because of impossibility
Ca: And
Niravayavatvāt: Due to partlessness

Brahman is indivisible and formless, so it cannot have parts or divisions within itself.

3.2.26 (344) – सूक्ष्मत्वात्तु तद्धर्मवत् (Sūkṣmatvāttu Taddharmavat)

Due to its subtlety, it possesses such attributes.

Sūkṣmatvāt: Due to subtlety
Tu: But
Taddharmavat: Possessing such attributes

The subtle nature of Brahman allows it to pervade
all existence and display attributes seen in creation.

———— • ◆ • ————

3.2.27 (345) – चाक्षुषत्वादन्यत्र न तथा हि दर्शयति
(Cākṣuṣatvādanyatra Na Tathā Hi Darśayati)

Not so elsewhere, as it does not display the same visibility.

Cākṣuṣatvāt: From visibility
Anyatra: Elsewhere
Na: Not
Tathā: So
Hi: Indeed
Darśayati: Displays

Brahman is not directly visible like physical objects;
its presence is inferred through effects and scriptures.

3.2.28 (346) – यथान्यत्र चात्र च श्रुतिः दृष्टाः चोपपत्तेः
(Yathānyatra Cātra Ca Śrutiḥ Dṛṣṭāḥ Copapatteḥ)

As in other contexts, so here too, this is supported by scriptures and reasoning.

Yathānyatra: As elsewhere |
Cātra: And here
Śrutiḥ: Scriptures
Dṛṣṭāḥ: Seen
Ca: And
Upapatteḥ: Logical reasoning

The scriptural and logical evidence that applies to other contexts also affirms Brahman's attributes here.

———— · ◆ · ————

3.2.29 (347) – अनुकम्पातु उपपत्तेः (Anukampātu Upapatteḥ)

But due to compassion, it is appropriate.

Anukampāt: From compassion
Tu: But
Upapatteḥ: Appropriate

Brahman's manifestation in creation stems from compassion, ensuring the sustenance of beings.

3.2.30 (348) – परिणामत्वं च शास्त्रात् (Pariṇāmatvaṁ Ca Śāstrāt)

Transformation is affirmed by scripture.

Pariṇāmatvam: Transformation
Ca: And
Śāstrāt: From scripture

The scriptures describe the world as a
transformation of Brahman, affirming its causal nature.

3.2.31 (349) – गुणकृतित्वं च गुणतः (Guṇakṛtitvaṁ Ca Guṇataḥ)

The performance of actions is due to qualities (of Prakriti).

Guṇakṛtitvam: Action due to qualities
Ca: And
Guṇataḥ: From qualities

The actions in creation are driven by the three gunas (qualities of nature)
inherent in Prakriti, while Brahman remains unaffected.

3.2.32 (350) – अत्र च तद्विज्ञानं प्रयोजनम्
(Atra Ca Tadvijñānaṁ Prayojanam)

Here, the purpose is the knowledge of that (Brahman).

Atra: Here
Ca: And
Tadvijñānam: Knowledge of that (Brahman)
Prayojanam: Purpose

The ultimate aim of scriptural study is to realize
Brahman, as knowledge alone leads to liberation.

3.2.33 (351) – अन्वर्थसंभवात्तद्व्यपदेशः
(Anvarthasaṁbhavāttadvyapadeśaḥ)

The name is appropriate due to its correspondence to the essence.

Anvartha: Correspondence to meaning
Saṁbhavāt: Due to possibility
Tadvyapadeśaḥ: Its designation

The terms used for Brahman in the scriptures are meaningful,
as they accurately describe its essence and attributes.

3.2.34 (352) – अभ्युपगमाच्च दोषवर्जित्वम्
(Abhyupagamācca Doṣavarjitvam)

And because it is admitted to be free from defects.

Abhyupagamāt: From admission
Ca: And
Doṣavarjitvam: Freedom from defects

Brahman is recognized as flawless and beyond imperfections, distinguishing it from all other entities.

· ◆ ·

3.2.35 (353) – असंशब्दिवदसामान्यशब्दवत्त्वं चोपपत्ते:
(Asaṁśabdivadasāmānyaśabdavattvaṁ Copapatteḥ)

**Like non-ordinary words, Brahman's
terms are appropriate due to its uniqueness.**

Asaṁśabdivat: Like uncommon terms
Asāmānyaśabdavattvam: Usage of non-ordinary words
Ca: And
Upapatteḥ: Due to reason

Words used for Brahman are extraordinary, signifying its unparalleled and unique nature.

3.2.36 (354) – अनर्थान्तरत्वं च वर्णनात् (Anarthāntaratvaṁ Ca Varṇanāt)

And because it is not different from its essence, as described.

Anarthāntaratvam: Non-difference from its essence
Ca: And
Varṇanāt: From description

Brahman's attributes and essence are identical,
as the scriptures do not describe it as separate from itself.

———— • ◆ • ————

3.2.37 (355) – सर्वत्र प्रकरणात्तद्व्यपदेशः
(Sarvatra Prakaraṇāttadvyapadeśaḥ)

Its designation is consistent across all contexts.

Sarvatra: Everywhere
Prakaraṇāt: From context
Tadvyapadeśaḥ: Its designation

Brahman is consistently described as the ultimate
reality across all scriptural contexts, affirming its unity.

3.2.38 (356) – तद्विकल्पोपदेशाच्य (Tadvikalpopadeśācca)

And because alternatives (to Brahman) are also taught.

Tadvikalpa: Alternatives to that (Brahman)
Upadeśāt: From teaching
Ca: And

Scriptures teach the alternatives (the manifested universe)
only to ultimately direct understanding toward Brahman.

———————— • ◆ • ————————

3.2.39 (357) – आपत्तिरुपपत्ते: (Āpattirūpapatteḥ)

Reconciliation is logical.

Āpattiḥ: Reconciliation
Upapatteḥ: Logical reasoning

Apparent contradictions in the scriptures are
resolved by recognizing Brahman as the substratum of all.

3.2.40 (358) – स्वरूपेण व्यक्तिर्नाभ्युपगम्यते
(Svarūpeṇa Vyaktirnābhyupagamyate)

Manifestation in its true form is not admitted.

Svarūpeṇa: In true form
Vyaktiḥ: Manifestation
Na: Not
Abhyupagamyate: Admitted

Brahman's true nature is not directly perceivable; it is only known through inference and scriptural teachings.

3.2.41 (359) – परिणामादन्यथानुपपत्तेः च
(Pariṇāmādanyathānupapatteśca)

Transformation and the impossibility of any other explanation confirm it.

Pariṇāmāt: From transformation
Anyathā: Otherwise
Anupapatteḥ: Impossibility
Ca: And

The concept of transformation and the lack of alternative explanations affirm that Brahman is the ultimate cause of the universe.

SECTION 3

(SUTRAS 360–425)

3.3.1 (360) – यथाश्रयभेदात् तदुपपत्तेः (Yathāśrayabhedāt Tadupapatteḥ)

As there is a difference in substratum, the conclusion is appropriate.

Yathā: As
Āśrayabhedāt: Due to difference in substratum
Tadupapatteḥ: That conclusion is logical

The nature of worship varies depending on the substratum, reflecting the diversity in scriptural teachings about meditation and devotion.

3.3.2 (361) – उपपन्नं च वन्नतः (Upapannaṁ Ca Vannataḥ)

It is appropriate, as stated in the scriptures.

Upapannaṁ: Appropriate
Ca: And
Vannataḥ: As stated

The scriptural instructions are consistent with the context and purpose of meditation, ensuring harmony in their application.

3.3.3 (362) – अन्यत्राभावाच्य (Anyatrābhāvācca)

Because of the absence of (contradictions) elsewhere.

Anyatra: Elsewhere
Abhāvāt: Absence
Ca: And

The conclusions drawn about Brahman and meditation
are consistent and uncontradicted in other scriptural sections.

--- • ◆ • ---

3.3.4 (363) – तथा च दर्शयति (Tathā Ca Darśayati)

And so, it is demonstrated.

Tathā: So
Ca: And
Darśayati: Demonstrates

Scriptures explicitly demonstrate the consistency and relevance
of meditative practices aligned with the realization of Brahman.

3.3.5 (364) – उपदेशादधिगमः (Upadeśādadhigamaḥ)

Knowledge arises from teaching.

Upadeśāt: From teaching
Adhigamaḥ: Knowledge

The realization of Brahman is attained through the teachings of the scriptures, highlighting the importance of guidance from authoritative texts.

———————— • ◆ • ————————

3.3.6 (365) – संप्रसादादेव च ततः (Saṁprasādādeva Ca Tataḥ)

And indeed, from serenity itself, knowledge follows.

Saṁprasādāt: From serenity
Eva: Indeed
Ca: And
Tataḥ: From that

A calm and serene mind is essential for attaining knowledge of Brahman, as affirmed by the scriptures.

3.3.7 (366) – स्मृत्यनवकाशो हि प्रमाणाभावात्
(Smṛtyanavakāśo Hi Pramāṇābhāvāt)

**Smti (secondary scripture) has
no room here due to lack of authority.**

Smṛtyanavakāśaḥ: No scope for Smṛti
Hi: Indeed
Pramāṇābhāvāt: Due to lack of authority

Smṛti cannot overrule the primary scriptures (Śruti)
when it comes to meditative and spiritual practices.

3.3.8 (367) – त्रैविधानुपपत्तेश्च (Traividhānupapatteśca)

Because of the impossibility of the threefold difference.

Traividhānupapatteḥ: Impossibility of threefold difference
Ca: And

The distinctions of worship, meditative practice, and knowledge
are unified in their purpose, avoiding unnecessary divisions.

3.3.9 (368) – स्थित्युपपत्तेश्चाप्येषां द्वैतम्
(Sthityupapatteścāpyeṣāṁ Dvaitam)

**And because of the appropriateness
of their coexistence, duality exists.**

Sthityupapatteḥ: From appropriateness of coexistence
Ca: And
Api: Also
Eṣāṁ: Their
Dvaitam: Duality

The duality of the individual soul and Brahman is
acceptable in specific contexts, such as meditation and worship.

3.3.10 (369) – त्रैविध्यं चाभेदनियमात् (Traividhyaṁ Cābhedaniyamāt)

The threefold division is valid due to the rule of non-difference.

Traividhyam: Threefold division
Ca: And
Abhedaniyamāt: From the rule of non-difference

Even within the apparent distinctions in practices,
there remains an underlying unity rooted in Brahman.

3.3.11 (370) – अन्वयव्यासाभ्यां च (Anvayavyāsābhyāṁ Ca)

Because of agreement and difference, too.

Anvaya: Agreement
Vyāsa: Difference
Abhyāṁ: By both
Ca: And

Both agreement (identity of essence) and difference (manifestations) are acknowledged in the relationship between the individual soul and Brahman.

3.3.12 (371) – उपसंग्रहाच्च (Upasaṁgrahācca)

And because it is included.

Upasaṁgrahāt: From inclusion
Ca: And

The individual soul is included in Brahman, highlighting their essential unity despite apparent distinctions.

3.3.13 (372) – न च कल्पनायामपि प्राप्तिः (Na Ca Kalpanāyāmapi Prāptiḥ)

And even in the imagined, there is no attainment.

Na: Not
Ca: And
Kalpanāyām: In imagination
Api: Even
Prāptiḥ: Attainment

The imagined distinctions between the individual soul
and Brahman do not hinder the ultimate realization of unity.

—— · ◆ · ——

3.3.14 (373) – साक्षाच्चोभयम् (Sākṣaccobhayam)

Both (direct and indirect knowledge) are valid.

Sākṣāt: Direct
Ca: And
Ubhayam: Both

Both direct perception and scriptural
teachings are essential for understanding Brahman.

3.3.15 (374) – कार्यकरणात्मकत्वात् तु तद्विभागः
(Kāryakaraṇātmakatvāt Tu Tadvibhāgaḥ)

The distinction is due to the functions of cause and effect.

Kārya: Effect
Karaṇa: Cause
Ātmakatvāt: Being of the nature of
Tu: However
Tadvibhāgaḥ: Its distinction

The apparent separation between the soul and Brahman arises because of their roles as effect and cause, respectively.

———— • ◆ • ————

3.3.16 (375) – लोकवदुपलब्धेः (Lokavadupalabdheḥ)

As perceived in the world.

Lokavat: Like the world
Upalabdheḥ: From observation

Just as cause and effect are seen in worldly phenomena, so too is the relationship between Brahman and the universe understood.

3.3.17 (376) – सत्यानृते मिथुनीकृते (Satyānṛte Mithunīkṛte)

Truth and falsehood are mingled.

Satya: Truth
Anṛte: Falsehood
Mithunīkṛte: Are mingled

The individual soul reflects both reality
(as a part of Brahman) and illusion (due to ignorance).

———— • ♦ • ————

3.3.18 (377) – व्यतिरेकाच्च (Vyatirekācca)

And also due to separateness.

Vyatirekāt: From separateness
Ca: And

The separateness of the soul from Brahman in certain contexts
is necessary for understanding its limitations and ultimate liberation.

3.3.19 (378) – संकल्पाधिकरणे चायः (Saṁkalpādhikaraṇe Cāyaḥ)

And in the case of resolution, too, it applies.

Saṁkalpa: Resolution
Ādhikaraṇe: In the context of
Ca: And
Ayaḥ: It applies

The soul's resolutions and desires are distinct but ultimately
lead to realization of its unity with Brahman.

3.3.20 (379) – अनिर्देश्यात्वान्नान्यार्थं (Anirdeśyatvānnānyārthaṁ)

Due to indefiniteness, it does not mean something else.

Anirdeśyatvāt: Due to indefiniteness
Na: Not
Anyārtham: Refers to something else

The indefiniteness in the scriptures about the soul
points to its identity with Brahman, not to any other entity.

3.3.21 (380) – अपि च प्राणदिषु स्थानमं (Api Ca Prāṇādiṣu Sthānamaṁ)

nd also, in breath and others, it has its seat.

Api: Also
Ca: And
Prāṇādiṣu: In breath and others
Sthānam: Its seat

Brahman pervades even subtle elements like
breath, showing its all-encompassing nature.

3.3.22 (381) – मुख्यतस्त्वनुस्मृतिः (Mukhyatastvanusmṛtiḥ)

But the principal (meditation) is remembered.

Mukhyataḥ: Principally
Tu: But
Anusmṛtiḥ: Is remembered

In the context of meditation, the primary focus on Brahman
is emphasized and repeatedly recalled for ultimate realization.

3.3.23 (382) – स्थानं तद्व्यपदेशात् चात्र ह्येवंप्राप्ति:
(Sthānaṁ Tadvyapadeśāt Cātra Hyevaṁprāptiḥ)

**The seat (of the soul) is due to the
declaration, for this is the conclusion.**

Sthānam: Seat
Tadvyapadeśāt: Due to declaration of that
Ca: And
Atra: Here
Hi: For
Evaṁprāptiḥ: This is the conclusion

The scriptures declare that the seat of the soul lies within
Brahman, reinforcing its ultimate connection to the Supreme.

———————— • ♦ • ————————

3.3.24 (383) – अन्त:प्रविष्टश्च ध्रुवं श्रद्धानुमानभ्याम्
(Antaḥpraviṣṭaśca Dhruvaṁ Śraddhānumānabhyām)

**And (Brahman) has entered within,
undoubtedly, as inferred by faith and reasoning.**

Antaḥpraviṣṭaḥ: Entered within
Ca: And
Dhruvaṁ: Certainly
Śraddhā: Faith
Anumānabhyām: By reasoning

Faith and reasoning support the idea that Brahman
pervades everything internally and externally.

3.3.25 (384) – पञ्चवृत्तिः प्रमाणतश्च (Pañcavṛttiḥ Pramāṇataśca)

(Meditation includes) five functions, as proven by evidence.

Pañcavṛttiḥ: Five functions
Pramāṇataḥ: From evidence
Ca: And

The meditation processes involve five functions—hearing, reflecting, meditating, discriminating, and stabilizing—each supported by scriptural evidence.

— ◆ —

3.3.26 (385) – न च प्रतिकर्मणि सामान्यशब्दाच्छब्दविशेषात् (Na Ca Pratikarmaṇi Sāmānyaśabdācchabdaviśeṣāt)

Not in (every) action, as the general terms (are clarified by) specific words.

Na: Not
Ca: And
Pratikarmaṇi: In every action
Sāmānyaśabdāt: From general words
Śabdaviśeṣāt: By specific words

General references in the scriptures are refined by specific instructions, ensuring precision in meditative practices.

3.3.27 (386) – आश्रमकर्मा मुख्यं तु बलेन तथैव हि
(Āśramakarmā Mukhyaṁ Tu Balena Tathaiva Hi)

The duties of the stages of life are primary, as they are binding.

Āśramakarmā: Duties of stages of life
Mukhyaṁ: Primary
Tu: But
Balena: By obligation
Tathaiva: Just so
Hi: Indeed

The prescribed duties of different life stages hold primary importance as they form the foundation for spiritual progress.

* ◆ *

3.3.28 (387) – उपसंग्रहार्थं तु तद्वद्विधानात्
(Upasagrahrtha Tu Tadvadvidhnt)

But for the sake of inclusion, it is ordained similarly.

Upasaṁgrahārthaṁ: For the sake of inclusion
Tu: But
Tadvadvidhānāt: Ordained similarly

Similar meditative techniques are included to unify diverse practices, ensuring consistency in spiritual disciplines.

3.3.29 (388) – नास्ति तु तद्भाक्तं विशिष्टफलत्वात्
(Nāsti Tu Tadbhāktaṁ Viśiṣṭaphalatvāt)

But that (secondary result) does not exist, as the result is specific.

Nāsti: Does not exist
Tu: But
Tadbhāktaṁ: Secondary result
Viśiṣṭaphalatvāt: Due to specific result

Secondary outcomes of meditation are not the focus,
as the ultimate result—realization of Brahman—is paramount.

———————— • ◆ • ————————

3.3.30 (389) – गुणानामात्मनः श्रुतेः च तत्र यथाश्रयं तु
(Guṇānāmātmanaḥ Śruteś Ca Tatra Yathāśrayaṁ Tu)

**The qualities of the Self (are understood) from
the scriptures according to the substratum.**

Guṇānām: Of qualities
Ātmanaḥ: Of the Self
Śruteḥ: From the scriptures
Ca: And
Tatra: There
Yathāśrayaṁ: According to substratum
Tu: But

The scriptures explain the qualities of the
Self based on the specific context and substratum of reference.

3.3.31 (390) – स्थितानां च गुणेषु तद्वद्विधानात्
(Sthitānāṁ Ca Guṇeṣu Tadvadvidhānāt)

And of those qualities abiding, it is similarly prescribed.

Sthitānām: Of those abiding
Ca: And
Guṇeṣu: In qualities
Tadvadvidhānāt: Similarly prescribed

The enduring qualities of the Self are similarly addressed in meditative and scriptural practices, ensuring continuity of understanding

———— • ◆ • ————

3.3.32 (391) – गुणदोषव्यपदेशेषु धर्मोपपत्तेः
(Guṇadoṣavyapadeśeṣu Dharmopapatteḥ)

In references to merits and demerits, righteousness is explained.

Guṇadoṣa: Merits and demerits
Vyapadeśeṣu: In references
Dharma: Righteousness
Upapatteḥ: Is explained

Scriptures discuss the interplay of virtues and flaws to elucidate the path of righteousness and its implications for liberation.

3.3.33 (392) – असंभवस्तु सतः श्रुतेः (Asaṁbhavastu Sataḥ Śruteḥ)

However, impossibility is for the existent, as stated in the scriptures.

Asaṁbhavaḥ: Impossibility
Tu: But
Sataḥ: Of the existent
Śruteḥ: From the scriptures

The scriptures clarify that certain contradictions, like the creation of existence from non-existence, are not possible within the realm of Brahman.

3.3.34 (393) – स्यात्परमर्थत्वात् (Syātparamārthatvāt)

It exists as the ultimate reality.

Syāt: Exists
Paramārthatvāt: As ultimate reality

Brahman is the sole ultimate reality, transcending all material illusions and dualities.

3.3.35 (394) – उपमर्दं चाल्पक्षयात् (Upamardaṁ Cālpakṣayāt)

And destruction (of the illusory world) occurs due to its slightness.

Upamardaṁ: Destruction
Ca: And
Alpakṣayāt: Due to slightness

The illusory nature of the world is easily overcome
or destroyed upon realization of Brahman's ultimate truth.

———— • ♦ • ————

3.3.36 (395) – प्रकरणात् तु विशेषणव्यपदेश:
(Prakaraṇāt Tu Viśeṣaṇavyapadeśaḥ)

But, due to context, the specific description (is appropriate).

Prakaraṇāt: Due to context
Tu: But
Viśeṣaṇavyapadeśaḥ: Specific description

The context in scriptures determines the use of specific
terms and descriptions to clarify subtle aspects of Brahman.

3.3.37 (396) – न तु कारणत्वाभावात् (Na Tu Kāraṇatvābhāvāt)

Not so, as there is no absence of causality.

Na: Not
Tu: But
Kāraṇatvābhāvāt: Due to absence of causality

Brahman remains the ultimate cause of
creation and sustains its causal relationship throughout.

————— • ◆ • —————

3.3.38 (397) – भूतान्यथान्यथात्वं च प्रकरणाद्विशेषितम्
(Bhūtānyathānyathātvaṁ Ca Prakaraṇādviśeṣitam)

The nature of beings varies accordingly and is defined by context.

Bhūtānyathānyathātvaṁ: Changing nature of beings
Ca: And
Prakaraṇāt: By context
Viśeṣitam: Defined

The nature of beings, as described in scriptures,
shifts according to their context and role within the cosmic order.

3.3.39 (398) – तद्दृष्टेः संसर्गं चान्यथा (Taddṛṣṭeḥ Saṁsargaṁ Cānyathā)

From that perspective, association is different.

Taddṛṣṭeḥ: From that perspective
Saṁsargaṁ: Association
Ca: And
Anyathā: Different

The scriptural vision distinguishes Brahman's transcendental association from worldly relationships.

3.3.40 (399) – विशुद्धं च ज्ञेयम् (Viśuddhaṁ Ca Jñeyam)

And the pure (Self) is to be known.

Viśuddham: The pure
Ca: And
Jñeyam: To be known

Knowledge of the pure and untainted nature of the Self is essential for spiritual realization.

3.3.41 (400) – न च तद्वदनुमानं (Na Ca Tadvadanumānaṁ)

Nor is inference (like direct scriptural evidence).

Na: Not
Ca: And
Tadvad: Like that
Anumānaṁ: Inference

Inference cannot replace direct knowledge derived
from scriptures when understanding Brahman's nature..

———— • ♦ • ————

3.3.42 (401) – अभिसन्धिसमायुक्तस्य च
(Abhisandhisamāyuktasya Ca)

And (only) for one who is associated with intention.

Abhisandhi: Intention
Samāyuktasya: Of one associated with
Ca: And

Scriptural instructions are effective only for those who
approach with a focused and sincere intent toward realization.

3.3.43 (402) – यथा चित्तं तथा च (Yathā Cittaṁ Tathā Ca)

And as is the mind, so it (results).

Yathā: As
Cittaṁ: The mind
Tathā: So
Ca: And

The spiritual outcome aligns with the nature and state
of one's mind, emphasizing the importance of purity and focus.

———— • ◆ • ————

3.3.44 (403) – परिणामदर्शनाच्च (Pariṇāmadarśanācca)

And because of the evidence of transformation.

Pariṇāma: Transformation
Darśanāt: Evidence
Ca: And

The visible transformations in spiritual practices and life
experiences point to the effectiveness of sustained effort and intention.

3.3.45 (404) – श्रुतेस्तु नार्थात्मकत्वात् (Śrutestu Narthtmakatvt)

From scripture, not (merely) as a material entity.

Śruteḥ: From scripture
Tu: But
Na: Not
Arthātmakatvāt: As a material entity

The scriptures reveal Brahman as transcendental
and not confined to any material aspect.

———— • ♦ • ————

3.3.46 (405) – विशुद्धोपदेशाच्य (Viśuddhopadeśācca)

And because of instructions regarding purity.

Viśuddha: Pure
Upadeśāt: Instruction
Ca: And

The teachings stress purity of thought, deed,
and understanding as prerequisites for Brahman realization.

3.3.47 (406) – कर्मणां प्रभावात् च (Karmaṇāṁ Prabhāvāt Ca)

And because of the influence of actions.

Karmaṇāṁ: Of actions |
Prabhāvāt: Influence
Ca: And

Actions performed with devotion and alignment to
dharma significantly impact one's spiritual progress.

———————— • ◆ • ————————

3.3.48 (407) – न साङ्कर्यमेव तु (Na Sāṅkaryameva Tu)

Not mere intermingling, but indeed (a higher purpose).

Na: Not
Sāṅkaryam: Intermingling
Eva: Indeed
Tu: But

The process of spiritual evolution is not arbitrary
but follows a higher purpose and divine order.

3.3.49 (408) – परं च श्रुतेः (Param Ca ŚShruteḥ)

And beyond (the material realm), as per the scriptures.

Param: Beyond
Ca: And
Śruteḥ: From scripture

Brahman transcends all material and
perceptible realms, as explicitly declared in the scriptures.

———— • ♦ • ————

3.3.50 (409) – चित्तस्य तन्त्रोऽनुकूलः (Cittasya Tantro'nukūlaḥ)

The mind's movement is aligned with intention.

Cittasya: Of the mind
Tantraḥ: Movement
Anukūlaḥ: Aligned

The disciplined mind aligns with higher
intentions, facilitating spiritual progress.

3.3.51 (410) – उभयप्राप्तौ सन्ध्ये स्यात् (Ubhayaprāptau Sandhye Syāt)

In the intermediate state, both are possible.

Ubhayaprāptau: On attaining both
Sandhye: In the intermediate state
Syāt: Is possible

The seeker in the transitional state can access both material and spiritual realms before ultimate liberation.

———— · ◆ · ————

3.3.52 (411) – यथा श्रुतिर्हि दर्शनात् (Yathā Śrutirhi Darśanāt)

As scripture declares and perception confirms.

Yathā: As
Śrutiḥ: Scripture
Hi: Indeed
Darśanāt: By perception

Scriptures and direct experiences harmoniously validate spiritual truths.

3.3.53 (412) – उपसंहारात् च (Upasaṁhārāt Ca)

And due to the conclusion.

Upasaṁhārāt: From the conclusion
Ca: And

The conclusions drawn in the scriptures affirm
the unified nature of Brahman and its teachings.

––––––––––– • ◆ • –––––––––––

3.3.54 (413) – अनुपलब्धेः संभवः (Anupalabdheḥ Saṁbhavaḥ)

Non-attainment (of liberation) is possible (in certain cases).

Anupalabdheḥ: Non-attainment
Saṁbhavaḥ: Is possible

Liberation may not be attained if the seeker
lacks essential qualities or proper practice.

3.3.55 (414) – अधिगमः प्रवृत्तेः स्यात् (Adhigamaḥ Pravṛtteḥ Syāt)

Realization occurs through effort.

Adhigamaḥ: Realization
Pravṛtteḥ: Through effort
Syāt: Occurs

Steady and focused effort in spiritual practices leads to realization.

3.3.56 (415) – व्यवधानं हि द्रष्टव्यम् (Vyavadhānaṁ Hi Draṣṭavyam)

Indeed, obstacles are to be identified.

Vyavadhānaṁ: Obstacles
Hi: Indeed
Draṣṭavyam: To be identified

Recognizing and addressing barriers on
the spiritual path is essential for progress.

3.3.57 (416) – विभागादेव च (Vibhāgādeva Ca)

And indeed, because of distinction.

Vibhāgāt: Due to distinction
Eva: Indeed
Ca: And

Liberation involves distinguishing the self
from the non-self, leading to true understanding.

———— • ♦ • ————

3.3.58 (417) – उपदेशादेव च (Upadeśādeva Ca)

And indeed, from instructions.

Upadeśāt: From instructions
Eva: Indeed
Ca: And

The teachings of scriptures provide a clear guide
to recognize the truth and achieve liberation.

3.3.59 (418) – उपपत्तेश्च (Upapatteśca)

And also from reasoning.

Upapatteḥ: From reasoning
Ca: And

Reasoning supports scriptural teachings, reinforcing
the truths of Brahman and the path to liberation.

———— • ◆ • ————

3.3.60 (419) – असंशयाच्च (Asaṁśayācca)

And because there is no doubt.

Asaṁśayāt: Because of no doubt
Ca: And

When scripture, reason, and experience align,
there is no doubt about the reality of Brahman.

3.3.61 (420) – क्रियायोगात् च नित्यता (Kriyāyogāt Ca Nityatā)

Permanence is due to consistent practice.

Kriyāyogāt: Due to consistent practice
Ca: And
Nityatā: Permanence

The eternal nature of liberation is achieved
through steadfast spiritual practice and discipline.

3.3.62 (421) – साकाङ्क्षा तद्विदोपदेशात् (Sākāṅkṣā Tadvidopadet)

Aspiration arises from the teachings of the wise.

Sākāṅkṣā: Aspiration
Tadvidaḥ: Of the wise
Upadeśāt: From teachings

Guidance from enlightened teachers
inspires and directs seekers toward liberation.

3.3.63 (422) – असङ्गत्वान्न च अशब्दं (Asaṅgatvānna Ca Aśabdaṁ)

Because of non-attachment, it is not wordless.

Asaṅgatvāt: Due to non-attachment
Na: Not
Ca: And
Aśabdaṁ: Wordless

Although Brahman is unattached, its realization
is not beyond the scope of scriptures and teachings.

———————— • ◆ • ————————

3.3.64 (423) – प्रमाणतश्च तद्रूपं तद्भावात्
(Pramāṇataśca Tadrūpaṁ Tadbhāvāt)

The form (of realization) arises from proof and its nature.

Pramāṇataḥ: From proof
Ca: And
Tadrūpaṁ: That form
|Tadbhāvāt: From its nature

Realization of Brahman is substantiated by
scriptures and reasoning, reflecting its inherent nature.

3.3.65 (424) – दर्शनाच्य तत्सिद्धिः (Darśanācca Tatsiddhiḥ)

And realization arises from vision.

Darśanāt: From vision
Ca: And
Tatsiddhiḥ: That realization

The direct perception or vision of truth
leads to the ultimate realization of Brahman.

3.3.66 (425) – न विकल्पो धर्मवत् (Na Vikalpo Dharmavat)

There is no variation, as with dharma.

Na: Not
Vikalpaḥ: Variation
Dharmavat: As with dharma

The nature of liberation remains uniform and
unchanging, unlike variable worldly dharmas.

SECTION 4

(SUTRAS 426–477)

3.4.1 (426) – अपि संरेमः (Api Saṁremaḥ)

Indeed, there is also the conjunction (of Jiva with Brahman).

Api: Indeed
Saṁremaḥ: Conjunction

This sutra emphasizes the intimate connection between
the individual soul (Jiva) and the Supreme Soul (Brahman),
highlighting the unity despite apparent duality.

——————— • ◆ • ———————

3.4.2 (427) – दृष्टश्च (Dṛṣṭaśca)

And this is seen.

Dṛṣṭaḥ: Seen
Ca: And

Scriptures and experience both affirm the
union of Jiva and Brahman, indicating its veracity.

3.4.3 (428) – न स्थानविपर्ययात् (Na Sthānaviparyayāt)

Not due to displacement.

Na: Not
Sthānaviparyayāt: Due to displacement

The realization of unity with Brahman is not a physical relocation but a shift in understanding and perception.

———— · ◆ · ————

3.4.4 (429) – स्वरुपेणविभक्तः (Svarūpeṇavibhaktaḥ)

Differentiated in essence.

Svarūpeṇa: In essence
Vibhaktaḥ: Differentiated

Though Jiva appears distinct, its essential nature remains connected to the Supreme Brahman.

3.4.5 (430) – स्मृतेश्च (Smṛteśca)

And because of memory.

Smṛteḥ: Memory
Ca: And

Scriptures remind us of the eternal connection between Jiva and Brahman, strengthening faith in their unity.

------ • ♦ • ------

3.4.6 (431) – विवेकाच्च न विवादः (Vivekācca Na Vivādaḥ)

Due to discrimination, there is no contradiction.

Vivekāt: Due to discrimination
Ca: And
Na: Not
Vivādaḥ: Contradiction

With the proper understanding of the scriptures, contradictions about Jiva and Brahman dissolve.

3.4.7 (432) – अन्यथानुमानात् (Anyathānumānāt)

Otherwise, inference would contradict.

Anyathā: Otherwise
Anumānaḥ: Inference
At: From

Logical inference supports the unity of Jiva and Brahman, leaving no room for contradictory interpretations.

———— • ♦ • ————

3.4.8 (433) – प्रसिद्धेश्च (Prasiddheśca)

And because of established truth.

Prasiddheḥ: Established truth
Ca: And

The eternal connection between Jiva and Brahman is well-established in the Upanishads and cannot be denied.

3.4.9 (434) – उपलब्धेश्च (Upalabdheśca)

And because of realization.

Upalabdheḥ: Realization
Ca: And

Personal experience and realization confirm the teachings
of scriptures regarding the unity of Jiva and Brahman.

3.4.10 (435) – न कारणत्वात् (Na Kāraṇatvāt)

Not because it is the cause.

Na: Not
Kāraṇatvāt: Due to causality

The Supreme Brahman is not merely a cause in the
worldly sense but the ultimate reality behind all existence.

3.4.11 (436) – प्रकरणाच्च (Prakaraṇācca)

And because of the context.

Prakaraṇāt: From the context
Ca: And

The teachings of the scriptures about the unity of Jiva and
Brahman are consistent when understood within the proper context.

———— •◆• ————

3.4.12 (437) – स्मार्यते च (Smāryate Ca)

And it is also remembered.

Smāryate: It is remembered
Ca: And

Scriptures often remind us of the eternal truth of
Jiva's unity with Brahman, reinforcing the concept.

3.4.13 (438) – एवं चात्मशब्दात् (Evaṁ Cātmāśabdāt)

Thus also from the word "self".

Evaṁ: Thus
Ca: And
Ātmāśabdāt: From the word "self"

The term "self" (Ātman) used in scriptures clearly signifies the unity of the individual soul with Brahman.

3.4.14 (439) – न तु द्रष्टारमुपगृह्णाति (Na Tu Draṣṭāramupagṛhṇāti)

But it does not apprehend the seer.

Na: Not
Tu: But
Draṣṭāram: The seer
Upagṛhṇāti: Apprehends

The individual soul cannot grasp the ultimate seer (Brahman), as it transcends all comprehension.

3.4.15 (440) – प्रत्यगात्मन्येव चमद्द्वयात्
(Pratyagātmanyeva Camadvayāt)

And because the non-dual resides only in the inner self.

Pratyagātmanyeva: In the inner self only
Ca: And
Advayāt: Due to non-duality

The realization of Brahman as non-dual is
experienced within the inner self (Pratyagātman).

———— • ♦ • ————

3.4.16 (441) – गुणदोषविधिशब्दैक्यमविरोधः
(Guṇadoṣavidhiśabdaikyamavirodhaḥ)

**There is no contradiction in the
unity of qualities, defects, and injunctions.**

Guṇa: Quality
Doṣa: Defect
Vidhi: Injunction
Śabda: Word
Aikyam: Unity
Avirodhaḥ: No contradiction

Scriptural teachings regarding qualities, defects, and injunctions
are harmonious and lead to the same understanding of Brahman.

3.4.17 (442) – औपनिषदं प्रकरणं विशेषात्
(Āupaniṣadaṁ Prakaraṇaṁ Viśeṣāt)

The topic pertains specifically to the Upanishadic teachings.

Āupaniṣadam: Related to the Upanishads
Prakaraṇam: Topic
Viśeṣāt: Due to specificity

The teachings regarding the unity of Jiva and
Brahman are uniquely established through the Upanishads.

———— • ♦ • ————

3.4.18 (443) – परं जिज्ञास्यम् (Paraṁ Jijñāsyam)

The ultimate is to be inquired into.

Paraṁ: Ultimate
Jijñāsyam: To be inquired into

The true purpose of life is the inquiry into
and realization of Brahman, the ultimate reality.

3.4.19 (444) – नैवोपलब्धेः (Naivopalabdheḥ)

Not indeed due to perception.

Na: Not
Eva: Indeed
Upalabdheḥ: Due to perception

Brahman cannot be known through ordinary
perception but through higher spiritual knowledge.

———— • ♦ • ————

3.4.20 (445) – सत्त्वादन्यत्र दोषः (Sattvādanyatra Doṣaḥ)

Defect arises elsewhere due to the predominance of sattva.

Sattvāt: Due to sattva (purity)
Anyatra: Elsewhere
Doṣaḥ: Defect

Spiritual wisdom predominates in sattva but
must transcend to attain Brahman beyond qualities.

3.4.21 (446) – एकत्वं परस्य च श्रुतेः (Ekatvaṁ Parasya Ca Śruteḥ)

The unity of the Supreme is established in the scriptures.

Ekatvaṁ: Unity
Parasya: Of the Supreme
Ca: And
Śruteḥ: From the scriptures

The scriptures declare Brahman's
singular, undivided, and non-dual nature.

3.4.22 (447) – उपलब्धेः (Upalabdheḥ)

Because of perception (of unity).

Upalabdheḥ: Perception

The unity of Brahman and the individual soul
is realized through direct spiritual perception.

3.4.23 (448) – न चान्यसंबन्धः (Na Cānyasaṁbandhaḥ)

And there is no connection with anything else.

Na: Not
Ca: And
Anya: Other
Saṁbandhaḥ: Connection

Brahman remains unattached and
independent, untouched by anything else.

———— • ◆ • ————

3.4.24 (449) – कर्मणोऽव्यपदेशात्तथा हि दर्शयति
(Karmaṇo'vyapadeśāttathā Hi Darśayati)

Because action is not predicated, as thus it is shown.

Karmaṇaḥ: Action
Avyapadeśāt: Not predicated
Tathā: Thus
Hi: Indeed
Darśayati: Shows

Scriptures indicate that Brahman is beyond
action or doership, reaffirming its transcendent nature.

3.4.25 (450) – दृष्टश्च (Dṛṣṭaśca)

And it is seen (in the scriptures).

Dṛṣṭaḥ: Seen
Ca: And

The transcendence of Brahman is evident
in scriptural declarations and teachings.

———— · ◆ · ————

3.4.26 (451) – अनर्थक्यं च नेति चेन्न तत्
(Anarthakyaṁ Ca Neti Cenn Na Tat)

If it is said to be purposeless, that is not so.

Anarthakyaṁ: Purposelessness
Ca: And
Na: Not
Iti: Thus
Chet: If
Tat: That

The teachings of Brahman are not purposeless;
they serve as a guide to realizing the ultimate truth.

3.4.27 (452) – प्राज्ञवदवस्थानात् (Prājñavadavasthānāt)

Because it exists like the wise one (Prjña).

Prājña: Wise one
Avad: Like
Avasthānāt: Exists

Brahman exists in an all-knowing,
supreme state, untouched by ignorance or duality.

———————— · ♦ · ————————

3.4.28 (453) – ईक्षतेर्नाशब्दम् (Īkṣaternāśabdam)

Because of seeing, it is not without a name.

Īkṣateḥ: Because of seeing
Na: Not
Aśabdam: Without a name

Brahman is referred to in scriptures with
various names, signifying its presence and reality.

3.4.29 (454) – समानशब्दाच्च (Samānaśabdācca)

And because of similar terms.

Samāna: Similar
Śabdāt: Terms
Ca: And

The scriptures use consistent terminology to
describe Brahman, affirming its unity and singularity.

3.4.30 (455) – आप्तः शब्दोऽविसंवादात् (Āptaḥ Śabdo'visaṁvādāt)

The scriptures are authoritative
because they are free from contradiction.

Āptaḥ: Authoritative
Śabdaḥ: Scriptures
Avisaṁvādāt: Free from contradiction

The consistency and reliability of scriptural teachings
make them a trustworthy source for understanding Brahman.

3.4.31 (456) – भक्तित्वादुपदेशः स्यादिति चेन्न तत्स्थानात्
(Bhaktitvād Upadeśaḥ Syāditi Cenn Tatsthānāt)

**If it is argued that teaching would result
in limitation, that is not so because of its position.**

Bhaktitvāt: Limitation
Upadeśaḥ: Teaching
Syāt: Would result
Iti: Thus
Chet: If
Na: Not
Tatsthānāt: Because of its position

Teaching about Brahman does not impl
limitation, as it transcends all boundaries and positions.

———— • • ————

3.4.32 (457) – ब्रह्मवित्सर्वमप्नोति (Brahmavit Sarvam Apnoti)

The knower of Brahman attains everything.

Brahmavit: Knower of Brahman
Sarvam: Everything
Apnoti: Attains

The realization of Brahman leads to the ultimate
fulfillment and attainment of all that is desirable.

3.4.33 (458) – विज्ञाय प्राणादि लोकमप्येति स्तुत्यर्थः
(Vijñāya Prāṇādi Lokamapyeti Stutyarthaḥ)

Having known, one attains the worlds including that of Pra; it is for the purpose of eulogy.

Vijñāya: Having known
Prāṇādi: Including Prāṇa
Lokam: World
Apyeiti: Attains
Stutyarthaḥ: For the purpose of eulogy

The scriptures highlight the rewards of knowing Brahman to emphasize its supreme importance, though such rewards are secondary to self-realization.

3.4.34 (459) – शास्त्रदृष्यत्वात् (Śāstradṛṣṭyatvāt)

Because it is based on scriptural vision.

Śāstra: Scriptures
Dṛṣṭyatvāt: Based on vision

The teachings on attaining Brahman stem from
the divine vision of the scriptures, making them authoritative.

3.4.35 (460) – सर्वानुग्रहीत्वाच्च (Sarvānugrahītvācca)

And because it is the benefactor of all.

Sarva: All
Anugrahītvāt: Benefactor
Ca: And

Brahman's nature is to bless and uplift all beings, signifying its universal benevolence.

———— • ♦ • ————

3.4.36 (461) – प्रकरणाच्च (Prakaraṇācca)

And because of the context.

Prakaraṇāt: Context
Ca: And

The context of scriptural teachings confirms that the rewards are meant to inspire the seeker but do not limit Brahman's transcendence.

3.4.37 (462) – सर्ववेदान्तप्रतिज्ञाभ्यः (Sarvavedāntapratijñābhyaḥ)

From the declarations of all Vednta texts.

Sarva: All
Vedānta: Vedānta texts
Pratijñābhyaḥ: Declarations

All Vedānta texts unanimously declare Brahman
as the ultimate goal, confirming its supreme status.

————— •♦• —————

3.4.38 (463) – कार्ये चात्मा शास्त्रदृष्च्यत्वात्
(Kārye Cātmā Śāstradṛṣṭyatvāt)

**And the self is perceived in the
effects because of scriptural authority.**

Kārye: In the effects
Ca: And
Ātmā: Self
Śāstradṛṣṭyatvāt: Due to scriptural authority

The presence of Brahman can be perceived in
the manifested world, as declared by scriptures.

3.4.39 (464) – एवमप्युपमर्दः सम्पद्येत
(Evamapyupamardaḥ Sampadyeta)

Even so, destruction would occur.

Evam: Thus
Api: Even
Upamardaḥ: Destruction
Sampadyeta: Would occur

If Brahman were limited, it would lead to the destruction
of its supreme and infinite nature, which is not possible.

3.4.40 (465) – अनादित्वं च वक्तव्यम् (Anāditvaṁ Ca Vaktavyam)

Eternity must also be declared.

Anāditvaṁ: Eternity
Ca: Also
Vaktavyam: Must be declared

The eternal nature of Brahman is a fundamental
aspect of its reality, which scriptures consistently affirm.

3.4.41 (466) – अधिष्ठानं तु गच्छति (Adhiṣṭhānaṁ Tu Gacchati)

But the substratum remains.

Adhiṣṭhānaṁ: Substratum
Tu: But
Gacchati: Remains

Even when phenomena dissolve, the substratum
—Brahman—remains as the unchanging reality.

———— • ◆ • ————

3.4.42 (467) – लोकवत्तु लीघीयसी कारणात्
(Lokavattu Līghīyasī Kāraṇāt)

As in the world, due to a lighter cause.

Lokavat: As in the world
Tu: But
Līghīyasī: Lighter
Kāraṇāt: Cause

The manifestation of the world, like a dream,
arises from a subtle cause, ultimately rooted in Brahman.

3.4.43 (468) – न लोकवत्त्वं प्रधानत्वात् (Na Lokavattvaṁ Pradhānatvāt)

It is not like the world, because of the primacy (of Brahman).

Na: Not
Lokavattvaṁ: Like the world
Pradhānatvāt: Primacy

Unlike worldly phenomena, Brahman is supreme
and uncaused, making it fundamentally different.

3.4.44 (469) – साक्षाच्योभयदर्शिनः (Sākṣāṣāccobhayadarśinaḥ)

And directly so, for those who see both (aspects).

Sākṣāt: Directly
Ca: And
Ubhayadarśinaḥ: Those who see both

Realization of Brahman occurs directly for those who
perceive both its immanent and transcendent aspects.

3.4.45 (470) – अर्थवदनुपलब्धेः (Arthavadanupalabdheḥ)

As it is purposeful and not unperceived.

Arthavat: Purposeful
Anupalabdheḥ: Not unperceived

Brahman is purposeful and evident through spiritual realization, despite being beyond ordinary perception.

3.4.46 (471) – न च प्रज्ञा प्राप्तिः (Na Ca Prajñā Prāptiḥ)

And there is no attainment of wisdom.

Na: Not
Ca: And
Prajñā: Wisdom
Prāptiḥ: Attainment

Brahman is not attained through intellectual effort alone but through intuitive realization.

3.4.47 (472) – तस्मिन्नन्यत्मनः सम्भवात्
(Tasminnanyatmanaḥ Sambhavāt)

Because the individual self arises in It (Brahman).

Tasmin: In It (Brahman)
Anya: Different
Ātmanaḥ: Self
Sambhavāt: Arises

The individual self is a manifestation of
Brahman, existing within its ultimate reality.

—— • ◆ • ——

3.4.48 (473) – दृष्टश्चाव्यतिक्रमे (Dṛṣṭaścāvyatikrame)

And it is seen in the absence of transgression.

Dṛṣṭaḥ: Seen
Ca: And
Avyatikrame: Absence of transgression

Scriptural evidence confirms that the relationship between the
individual self and Brahman adheres to eternal laws without contradiction.

3.4.49 (474) – समकालत्वाच्च (Samakālatvācca)

And because they are simultaneous.

Samakālatvāt: Simultaneity
Ca: And

The individual self and Brahman coexist in
a timeless manner, emphasizing their inseparability.

———— • ◆ • ————

3.4.50 (475) – कर्तृविभागात् (Kartṛvibhāgāt)

Due to the division of the agent (and actions).

Kartṛ: Agent
Vibhāgāt: Division

The distinction between the doer and actions arises due to
ignorance, which is ultimately resolved in the realization of Brahman.

3.4.51 (476) – उपपत्तेः च (Upapatteḥ Ca)

And because it is reasonable.

Upapatteḥ: Reasonable
Ca: And

The unity of the individual self and Brahman
is logical and supported by philosophical reasoning.

———— • ♦ • ————

3.4.52 (477) – विशेषणाभावात् (Viśeṣaṇābhāvāt)

Because there is no distinction.

Viśeṣaṇa: Distinction
Abhāvāt: Absence

In the ultimate reality, all distinctions dissolve,
leaving only the non-dual nature of Brahman.

CHAPTER 4

◦ ◇ ◦

SECTION 1

(SUTRAS 478-496)

4.1.1 (478) – स्मर्यमाणेऽप्यविरोधः शेषवत्
(Smaryamāṇe'pyavirodhaḥ Śeṣavat)

Even when remembered, there is no contradiction, just as in the case of a remainder.

Smaryamāṇe: Being remembered
Api: Even
Avirodhaḥ: No contradiction
Śeṣavat: Like a remainder

This sutra emphasizes that even when certain aspects of Brahman are remembered or described, it does not conflict with its ultimate nature, just as remnants in other contexts do not alter the whole.

4.1.2 (479) – अनारम्भणशब्दोपपत्तेश्च (Anārambhaṇaśabdopapatteśca)

And because of the appropriateness of the term "non-origination."

Anārambhaṇa: Non-origination
Śabda: Word or term
Upapattesh: Appropriateness
Ca: And

Brahman is described as "not originating"
because it is eternal and uncreated, unlike the transient
and impermanent entities in the material world.

--- ◆ ---

4.1.3 (480) – तदात्मभेदव्यपदेशाच्य (Tadātmabhedavyapadeśācca)

And because of the statement of distinction from that self.

Tad: That
Ātma: Self
Bheda: Distinction
Vyapadeśāt: Statement of

The scriptures clearly distinguish between
the individual self and the supreme self, affirming that
Brahman is not limited or identical to the individual soul.

4.1.4 (481) – स्वरुपप्रतिषेधाच्य न विषयीकरणम्
(Svarūpapratiṣedhācca Na Viṣayīkaraṇam)

Because of the negation of nature, it cannot become an object.

Svarūpa: Nature
Pratiṣedhāt: Negation
Na: Not
Viṣayīkaraṇam: Objectification

Brahman cannot be objectified or fully comprehended, as its nature transcends all limitations and distinctions known to the human mind.

4.1.5 (482) – अनुभवाच्य (Anubhavācca)

And because of direct experience.

Anubhava: Direct experience
Ca: And

Brahman is realized not through intellectual understanding alone but through direct spiritual experience or self-realization.

4.1.6 (483) – विज्ञायतेऽन्यथाऽऽत्मशब्दात् (Vijñāyate'nyathā'tmaśabdāt)

It is understood differently from the term "self."

Vijñāyate: Understood
Anyathā: Differently
Ātma: Self
Śabdāt: From the term

Though Brahman is sometimes referred to as "self" in the scriptures, it is fundamentally different from the limited concept of the individual self.

— • ♦ • —

4.1.7 (484) – कारणत्वं च प्रविभागादन्येषाम्
(Kāraṇatvaṃ Ca Pravibhāgādanyeṣām)

The causal nature is assigned to others due to differentiation.

Kāraṇatvam: Causality
Ca: And
Pravibhāgāt: Differentiation
Anyeṣām: Of others

The causal nature of the universe is attributed to entities other than Brahman, as Brahman is beyond causality and differentiation.

4.1.8 (485) – लोकवत् तु लीलाकैवल्यम् (Lokavat Tu Līlākaivalyam)

But like in the world, it is mere playfulness.

Lokavat: Like in the world
Tu: But
Līlākaivalyam: Mere playfulness

The manifestation of the universe is seen as the play or
sport (līlā) of Brahman, without any binding necessity or motive.

4.1.9 (486) – तदन्यत्वमर्हन्तादिवदुक्तम् (Tadanyatvamarhantādivaduktam)

Its otherness is declared, as in the case of Arhats and others.

Tadanyatvam: Otherness
Arhantādi: Arhats and others
Uktam: Declared

Just as distinctions are made between Arhats and other beings,
the scriptures assert the separateness of Brahman from the
material and phenomenal realms.

4.1.10 (487) – उपपत्तेश्च (Upapatteśca)

And because it is reasonable.

Upapattes: Reasonable
Ca: And

The assertion of Brahman's transcendence and distinct
nature is logical and supported by reason as well as scripture.

————— • ◆ • —————

4.1.11 (488) – नैवमतः स्मर्यते (Naivamataḥ Smaryate)

It is not so, as remembered.

Na: Not
Evam: Thus
Ataḥ: Hence
Smaryate: Remembered

The scriptural descriptions of Brahman should not be misconstrued
as literal but understood in the context of their deeper, symbolic meaning.

4.1.12 (489) – तस्मादप्यनन्यभावः (Tasmādapyananyabhāvaḥ)

Therefore, even non-distinction exists.

Tasmāt: Therefore
Api: Even
Ananyabhāvaḥ: Non-distinction

Brahman is ultimately non-dual and beyond all distinctions,
despite apparent differences perceived in the phenomenal world.

————— • ◆ • —————

4.1.13 (490) – दर्शनाच्च (Darśanācca)

And because it is seen (in the scriptures).

Darśanāt: Seen
Ca: And

The non-dual nature of Brahman is supported by
direct references in the scriptures, which consistently
emphasize its unity and transcendence beyond duality.

4.1.14 (491) – सम्पत्त्यभिधानाच्च (Sampattyabhidhānācca)

And because of the declaration of merging.

Sampatti: Merging
Abhidhānāt: Declaration
Ca: And

The scriptures state that upon liberation,
the individual soul merges with Brahman, affirming its
ultimate oneness and inseparability from the supreme reality.

———— • ◆ • ————

4.1.15 (492) – श्रद्धाभेदात् च (Śraddhābhedāt Ca)

And because of the difference in faith.

Śraddhā: Faith
Bhedāt: Difference
Ca: And

The distinction between individual paths arises from
differences in faith and understanding, but these differences
dissolve when the ultimate reality of Brahman is realized.

4.1.16 (493) – वेद्यत्वं च न प्रथमम् (Vedyatvaṃ Ca Na Prathamam)

And it is knowable, but not initially.

Vedyatvam: Knowability
Ca: And
Na: Not
Prathamam: Initially

While Brahman is ultimately knowable,
its realization requires purification and spiritual progress;
it cannot be understood through mere intellectual effort at the outset.

———————— • ◆ • ————————

4.1.17 (494) – अद्वारेण तु निरदेशः (Advāreṇa Tu Niradeśaḥ)

But the description is indirect.

Advāreṇa: Indirectly
Tu: But
Niradeśaḥ: Description

Scriptures often describe Brahman indirectly through analogies
and negations, as it is beyond the scope of direct verbal expression.

4.1.18 (495) – नियमनात्तु (Niyamānattu)

But due to regulation.

Niyamāt: Regulation or discipline
Tu: But

The realization of Brahman requires discipline and
adherence to scriptural teachings, as it cannot be attained
without proper guidance and effort.

4.1.19 (496) – फलश्रुतेरित्युपपत्तिः (Phalaśruterityupapattiḥ)

Because of the mention of fruits, this is reasonable.

Phalaśruteḥ: Mention of fruits (results)
Iti: Thus
Upapattiḥ: Reasonable

The scriptures mention the fruits or results of spiritual practice to motivate
seekers, even though Brahman itself is beyond all results and causality.
This teaching is logically consistent within the framework of the scriptures.

SECTION 2

(SUTRAS 497–517)

4.2.1 (497) – आवृत्तिर्हि अशब्दम् (Āvṛttirhi Aśabdam)

Repetition is indeed implied by the absence of specific mention.

Āvṛttiḥ: Repetition
Hi: Indeed
Aśabdam: Absence of specific mention

Explanation: Spiritual practices, such as meditation or mantra repetition, are implied to be continuous, even when not explicitly stated in the scriptures, as they are essential for self-realization.

———— • ✦ • ————

4.2.2 (498) – समर्थानुवृत्तिरनुमानात् (Samarthānuvṛttiranumānāt)

Continuity is established from reasoning based on suitability.

Samarthā: Suitability
Anuvṛttiḥ: Continuity
Anumānāt: From reasoning

Continuity of spiritual disciplines is logically deduced because it is necessary for cultivating the required state of mind for realization.

4.2.3 (499) – त्रयाणामेव च मन्त्रोक्तम् (Trayāṇāmeva Ca Mantroktaṃ)

And only of the three, as stated in the mantras.

Trayāṇām: Of the three (paths)
Eva: Only
Ca: And
Mantroktaṃ: Stated in the mantras

The scriptures specify three primary paths—knowledge, devotion, and action—as the means to liberation, and these are affirmed in the mantras.

4.2.4 (500) – स्मृत्यनवकाशत्वाच्च (Smṛtyanavakāśatvācca)

Because otherwise, there would be no room for remembrance.

Smṛti: Remembrance
Anavakāśatvāt: Lack of room
Ca: And

Continuous practice is necessary, as without it, the mind would not have the stability or opportunity to retain the teachings and realize Brahman.

4.2.5 (501) – दृष्टं हि दर्शनात् (Dṛṣṭaṃ Hi Darśanāt)

Indeed, it is seen because of direct perception.

Dṛṣṭam: Seen or experienced
Hi: Indeed
Darśanāt: From direct perception

Direct experience of Brahman is possible through spiritual practices, as affirmed by scriptural descriptions and the testimonies of realized beings.

4.2.6 (502) – श्रुतेश्चेत्त्वमसंभवात् (Śruteścet Tvamasaṃbhavāt)

If it were based on scripture alone, it would not be possible.

Śruteḥ: From scripture
Cet: If
Tvam: You
Asaṃbhavāt: Impossibility

Realization cannot come solely through scriptural study;
direct experience and practice are essential, as theoretical knowledge
alone cannot lead to liberation.

4.2.7 (503) – तदेव च स्मरन्ति (Tadeva Ca Smaranti)

And that is what is remembered.

Tad: That
Eva: Only
Ca: And
Smaranti: Remember

The scriptures and teachings consistently emphasize the importance of sustained practice and remembrance as the means to realize Brahman.

———— • ♦ • ————

4.2.8 (504) – अथो यथार्थानुभवात् (Athoyathārthānubhavāt)

Because it results in a true experience of reality.

Athaḥ: Therefore
Yathārtha: True
Anubhavāt: Experience

Consistent spiritual practice culminates in the direct and true experience of Brahman, as revealed by the scriptures.

4.2.9 (505) – तत्समाप्तिश्च तदवसानात् (Tatsamāptiśca Tadavasānāt)

And its conclusion is in its cessation.

Tat: That
Samāptiḥ: Completion
Ca: And
Tadavasānāt: In its cessation

The culmination of spiritual practice is the cessation of ignorance and realization of the non-dual nature of Brahman.

———— • ◆ • ————

4.2.10 (506) – अपि च स्मर्यते (Api Ca Smaryate)

And indeed, it is also mentioned in the scriptures.

Api: Also
Ca: And
Smaryate: Mentioned

The scriptures support the importance of perseverance in practice, stating that liberation is achieved through unwavering focus and effort.

4.2.11 (507) – संशयमपि च हिनस्ति (Saṃśayamapi Ca Hinasti)

And it removes doubts.

Saṃśayam: Doubts
Api: Also
Ca: And
Hinasti: Removes

Sustained engagement with spiritual practices dispels doubts
and strengthens faith in the teachings, paving the way for liberation.

4.2.12 (508) – एवं च आत्मनि विद्यायां (Evaṃ Ca Ātmani Vidyāyām)

And thus, the knowledge of the Self.

Evaṃ: Thus
Ca: And
Ātmani: In the Self
Vidyāyām: In knowledge

The realization of the Self is achieved through the culmination of
meditative practices and adherence to scriptural teachings, which
unveil Brahman's nature.

4.2.13 (509) – यथाश्रुति न तु कथंचन (Yathāśruti Na Tu Kathañcana)

As per the scripture, and not otherwise.

Yathā: As
Śruti: Scripture
Na: Not
Tu: But
Kathañcana: In any way

Liberation must be sought in alignment with scriptural guidance, as it cannot be attained through arbitrary or unsupported methods.

4.2.14 (510) – साधनं च यथाश्रुतम् (Sādhanaṃ Ca Yathāśrutam)

The means (to liberation) is also as stated in the scriptures.

Sādhanaṃ: Means
Ca: And
Yathāśrutam: As heard

The prescribed practices such as meditation, devotion, and self-inquiry are validated by scriptural authority, forming the basis for attaining liberation.

4.2.15 (511) – स्मृतिसिद्धेः च यथार्थत्वम्
(Smṛtisiddheḥ Ca Yathārthatvam)

And the correctness of this is established through memory.

Smṛti: Memory
Siddheḥ: Establishment
Ca: And
Yathārthatvam: Correctness

The consistency of scriptural teachings with the recollections of realized sages validates the methods and outcomes of spiritual practice.

4.2.16 (512) – तस्मादेव च दृढनिष्ठा (Tasmādeva Ca Dṛḍhaniṣṭhā)

Therefore, unwavering focus (is necessary).

Tasmāt: Therefore
Eva: Only
Ca: And
Dṛḍhaniṣṭhā: Firm focus

Liberation demands unwavering commitment to the path prescribed by the scriptures, as distractions and doubt hinder progress.

4.2.17 (513) – उपसन्नस्य हि फलम् (Upasannasya Hi Phalam)

For one who is near (liberation), the fruit is assured.

Upasannasya: Of one who is near
Hi: Indeed
Phalam: Fruit

When a seeker earnestly approaches the Self with
sincere effort, the promised result of liberation is inevitable.

———— · ◆ · ————

4.2.18 (514) – समाहितस्य च फलश्रुतेः (Samāhitasya Ca Phalaśruteḥ)

And for the concentrated one, the fruit is stated.

Samāhitasya: Of one who is concentrated
Ca: And
Phalaśruteḥ: Mention of fruit

The scriptures affirm that for those who maintain a steady
and focused mind, liberation is both attainable and certain.

4.2.19 (515) – अधिगमः च श्रुत्यर्थतत्त्वात्
(Adhigamaḥ Ca Śrutyarthatattvāt)

And realization arises from
understanding the essence of the scriptures.

Adhigamaḥ: Realization
Ca: And
Śrutyarthatattvāt: From understanding the essence of scriptures

The knowledge imparted by the scriptures, when grasped
in its essence, leads directly to the realization of Brahman.

4.2.20 (516) – स्थितेः च इतरत्र न (Sthiteḥ Ca Itaratra Na)

And stability (in realization) does not exist elsewhere.

Sthiteḥ: Stability
Ca: And
Itaratra: Elsewhere
Na: Not

Stability in the knowledge of Brahman is achieved only through the
prescribed methods; alternative paths lack the necessary foundation.

4.2.21 (517) – इत्यवगमात् सर्वश्रुतिः समाप्तिः
(Ityavagamāt Sarvaśrutiḥ Samāptiḥ)

Thus, the conclusion of all the scriptures is known.

Iti: Thus
Avagamāt: From understanding
Sarvaśrutiḥ: All the scriptures
Samāptiḥ: Conclusion

The ultimate teaching of the scriptures is the realization
of non-dual Brahman as the ultimate truth, achieved through
faith, understanding, and practice.

SECTION 3

4.3.1 (518) – तदन्तरप्रतिपत्तेः (Tadantarapratipatteḥ)

(Liberation comes) immediately after the realization (of Brahman).

Tat: That (liberation)
Antara: Immediate
Pratipatteḥ: Realization

Explanation: Liberation follows instantly upon the true realization of Brahman, as the veil of ignorance is removed completely.

———— · ◆ · ————

4.3.2 (519) – स्मर्यते च तद्व्यपदेशः (Smaryate Ca Tadvyapadeśaḥ)

It is also mentioned as such in the scriptures.

Smaryate: Is remembered
Ca: And
Tadvyapadeśaḥ: Such a designation

Explanation: Scriptures confirm that liberation is achieved immediately upon attaining the knowledge of Brahman, with no further delay.

4.3.3 (520) – तदेव चात्मत्वात् (Tadeva Cātmatvāt)

And that alone (is true), because it is the Self.

Tad: That
Eva: Alone
Ca: And
Ātmatvāt: Being the Self

Liberation is instantaneous because Brahman is the innermost Self, and realization of this truth dissolves all duality.

———— • ◆ • ————

4.3.4 (521) – पूर्ववत् तथोपलब्धेः (Pūrvavat Tathopalabdheḥ)

As before, because it is so realized.

Pūrvavat: As before
Tathā: Thus
Upalabdheḥ: Realization

Just as the scriptures have described, liberation happens immediately upon realization, without any intervening actions.

4.3.5 (522) – उभयविधं च दोषविहीनम् (Ubhayavidhaṃ Ca Doṣavihīnam)

And it is of both types, devoid of defects.

Ubhayavidham: Of both types
Ca: And
Doṣavihīnam: Devoid of defects

Liberation is free from imperfections and applies both to those who attain it through gradual practice and those who achieve it immediately.

———— · ◆ · ————

4.3.6 (523) – परमार्थतश्च अविरोधः (Paramārthataśca Avirodhaḥ)

And ultimately, there is no contradiction.

Paramārthataḥ: Ultimately
Ca: And
Avirodhaḥ: No contradiction

From the ultimate standpoint, there is no contradiction in
the varying descriptions of liberation, as all lead to the same truth.

4.3.7 (524) – अनयोः प्रभावे स्यात् ततः तु तथात्वम्
(Anayoḥ Prabhāve Syāt Tataḥ Tu Tathātvam)

Of these two, the effect results in that state.

Anayoḥ: Of these two
Prabhāve: By the effect
Syāt: Results
Tataḥ: Then
Tu: But
Tathātvam: That state

Both direct and gradual paths culminate in the realization of the same truth, leading to the same state of liberation.

4.3.8 (525) – न च शेषत्वात् शेषस्य न तु गुणवत्
(Na Ca Śeṣatvāt Śeṣasya Na Tu Guṇavat)

It is not subordinate; it is not with qualities.

Na: Not
Ca: And
Śeṣatvāt: Subordination
Śeṣasya: Of the remainder
Guṇavat: With qualities

Liberation is not a subordinate state or tied to qualities. It is absolute and transcends all limitations.

4.3.9 (526) – तदस्ति च ततः ततः अपि च श्रुतेः
(Tadasti Ca Tataḥ Tataḥ Api Ca Śruteḥ)

And that exists, and also as stated in the scriptures.

Tadasti: That exists
Ca: And
Tataḥ: From there
Api: Also
Śruteḥ: From scripture

The existence of Brahman as the ultimate truth is affirmed by both reasoning and scriptural testimony.

———— • ◆ • ————

4.3.10 (527) – तस्मादेव च तद्वृद्धेः (Tasmādeva Ca Tadvṛddheḥ)

Therefore, that alone leads to its growth.

Tasmāt: Therefore
Eva: Alone
Ca: And
Tadvṛddheḥ: Its growth

The path of realization, as described in the scriptures, enhances the understanding and realization of Brahman.

4.3.11 (528) – स एव च सम्यक् प्रसादः (Sa Eva Ca Samyak Prasādaḥ)

And that alone is complete peace.

Sa: That
Eva: Alone
Ca: And
Samyak: Complete
Prasādaḥ: Peace

Liberation brings about perfect peace and contentment,
as it aligns one with the ultimate reality.

––––––– • ♦ • –––––––

4.3.12 (529) – नान्यथेत्यवगमात् (Nānyathetyavagamāt)

And not otherwise, as is understood.

Na: Not
Anyathā: Otherwise
Iti: Thus
Avagamāt: Understood

Liberation is achieved only through the realization of Brahman
as the non-dual reality, not through any other means.

4.3.13 (530) – सति हि स्वभावे तत्सिद्धिः (Sati Hi Svabhāve Tatsiddhiḥ)

Indeed, its attainment is in its inherent nature.

Sati: Being present
Hi: Indeed
Svabhāve: Inherent nature
Tatsiddhiḥ: Its attainment

Liberation is inherent to the nature of Brahman;
realization simply uncovers what already exists.

4.3.14 (531) – एकत्वं च यथाश्रुतम् (Ekatvaṃ Ca Yathāśrutam)

Oneness, as stated in the scriptures.

Ekatvaṃ: Oneness
Ca: And
Yathāśrutam: As stated

Liberation is the realization of oneness with
Brahman, a truth consistently affirmed in the scriptures.

4.3.15 (532) – अन्तःकरणस्य चैवम् (Antaḥkaraṇasya Caivam)

And so it is with the mind.

Antaḥkaraṇasya: Of the mind
Ca: And
Evam: Thus

The mind, when purified through discipline and knowledge,
reflects the reality of Brahman, leading to liberation.

4.3.16 (533) – ततः सति न चान्यः अपि च श्रुतेः
(Tataḥ Sati Na Cānyaḥ Api Ca Śruteḥ)

Then, indeed, there is no other; this is affirmed in the scriptures.

Tataḥ: Then
Sati: Indeed
Na: Not
Cānyaḥ: Another
Api: Also
Śruteḥ: By scripture

After realization, nothing other than Brahman exists,
as confirmed by scriptural declarations of non-duality.

SECTION 4

(SUTRAS 534–555)

4.4.1 (534) – समानाच्य (Samānācca)

And because of the sameness (of the ultimate goal).

Samāna: Sameness
Ca: And

Explanation: The ultimate goal of liberation is the same in all scriptural teachings, emphasizing the realization of Brahman.

———— · ◆ · ————

4.4.2 (535) – स्मृतेश्च (Smṛteśca)

And because of the scriptural memory.

Smṛteḥ: Scriptural memory
Ca: And

Explanation: The continuity of teachings in various scriptures reinforces the truth of attaining Brahman as the ultimate goal.

4.4.3 (536) – विकल्पा अपि हि गच्छन्ति (Vikalpā Api Hi Gacchanti)

Even those who follow alternative views ultimately reach (Brahman).

Vikalpā: Alternatives
Api: Even
Hi: Indeed
Gacchanti: Reach

Despite differences in practices or paths,
all sincere seekers ultimately attain Brahman.

4.4.4 (537) – आश्रयत्वात् (Āśrayatvāt)

Because it is the substratum.

Āśrayatvāt: Being the substratum

Brahman is the ultimate substratum of all existence,
making it the natural destination of all beings.

4.4.5 (538) – भोगं हि सह कार्यार्थोपपत्तेः
(Bhogaṁ Hi Saḥ Kāryārthopapatteḥ)

**Indeed, enjoyment is simultaneous
with the realization of the purpose.**

Bhogaṁ: Enjoyment
Hi: Indeed
Saḥ: That
Kāryārtha: Purpose of actions
Upapatteḥ: Appropriateness

Liberation involves supreme bliss, which is naturally
realized alongside the fulfillment of one's spiritual purpose.

———— • ◆ • ————

4.4.6 (539) – विज्ञप्तिस्वरूपत्वाच्च (Vijñaptisvarūpatvācca)

And because of its nature as pure consciousness.

Vijñapti: Consciousness
Svarūpatvāt: Nature
Ca: And

Brahman is pure consciousness, which is
fully experienced in the state of liberation.

4.4.7 (540) – अत एव च नित्यत्वम् (Ata Eva Ca Nityatvam)

Therefore, it is eternal.

Ata Eva: Therefore
Ca: And
Nityatvam: Eternity

The eternality of Brahman follows from its
nature as unchanging, limitless consciousness.

4.4.8 (541) – न च विकल्पस्य अधिकारः (Na Ca Vikalpasya Adhikāraḥ)

And there is no scope for alternatives.

Na: Not
Ca: And
Vikalpasya: Of alternatives
Adhikāraḥ: Scope

Once Brahman is realized, there is no room for
doubt or alternative interpretations regarding its nature.

4.4.9 (542) – असत्यमेव च (Asatyameva Ca)

And it is indeed unreal.

Asatyam: Unreal
Eva: Indeed
Ca: And

The world of duality is considered unreal
compared to the absolute reality of Brahman.

--- • ♦ • ---

4.4.10 (543) – अन्यथा च अप्युपपत्तेः (Anyathā Ca Apyupapatteḥ)

And otherwise too, it is appropriate.

Anyathā: Otherwise
Ca: And
Api: Also
Upapatteḥ: Appropriate

The realization of Brahman is reasonable and
consistent with the philosophical understanding of reality.

4.4.11 (544) – नन्दिष्यति हि (Nandiṣyati Hi)

Indeed, it will lead to bliss.

Nandiṣyati: Will lead to bliss
Hi: Indeed

Liberation naturally results in
unending bliss, as confirmed by the scriptures.

————— • ♦ • —————

4.4.12 (545) – अनुभूतिरिति च (Anubhūtiriti Ca)

And it is direct experience.

Anubhūtiḥ: Direct experience
Iti: Thus
Ca: And

Liberation is not a mere intellectual concept
but is experienced directly as the bliss of Brahman.

4.4.13 (546) – उभयात्मकत्वाच्च (Ubhayātmakatvācca)

And because it has the nature of both.

Ubhayātmakatvāt: Nature of both
Ca: And

Brahman encompasses both immanence and transcendence, reconciling all apparent contradictions.

4.4.14 (547) – अपि च स्वशक्त्यनुगृहीतः (Api Ca Svaśaktyanugṛhītaḥ)

And indeed, it is supported by its own power.

Api: Indeed
Ca: And
Svaśakty: Its own power
Anugṛhītaḥ: Supported

The realization of Brahman is facilitated by the divine power inherent within itself.

4.4.15 (548) – तदनुग्रहाय च (Tadanugrahāya Ca)

And for the grace of that (Brahman).

Tad: That (Brahman)
Anugrahāya: For grace
Ca: And

The grace of Brahman ensures the seeker's ultimate liberation.

———— ·◆· ————

4.4.16 (549) – आत्मप्रकाशत्वान्नियतिः (Ātmaprakāśatvānniyatiḥ)

Because the self is self-luminous, there is no limitation.

Ātmaprakāśatvāt: Due to self-luminosity
Niyatiḥ: Limitation

Brahman, being self-luminous and self-existent,
transcends all limitations and boundaries.

4.4.17 (550) – समानव्यपदेशाच्च (Samānavyapadeśācca)

And because of the common reference to sameness.

Samāna: Sameness
Vyapadeśāt: Reference
Ca: And

Scriptures consistently describe Brahman as the unchanging, ultimate reality, highlighting its uniformity across teachings.

4.4.18 (551) – अशब्दं च यत् (Aśabdaṁ Ca Yat)

And that which is beyond words.

Aśabdaṁ: Beyond words
Ca: And
Yat: That which

Brahman transcends linguistic description, being beyond words and conceptualization.

4.4.19 (552) – सूक्ष्मत्वाच्च (Sūkṣmatvācca)

And because of its subtlety.

Sūkṣmatvāt: Due to subtlety
Ca: And

Brahman's subtle nature makes it imperceptible
to ordinary senses, yet it pervades all existence.

4.4.20 (553) – आत्मप्राप्तिः फलम् (Ātmaprāptiḥ Phalam)

The attainment of the self is the ultimate result.

Ātmaprāptiḥ: Attainment of the self
Phalam: Result

Liberation culminates in realizing the self as
identical with Brahman, which is the highest goal.

4.4.21 (554) – अविशेषात् स्वभावस्य च (Aviśeṣāt Svabhāvasya Ca)

And because of the indivisibility of its nature.

Aviśeṣāt: Due to indivisibility
Svabhāvasya: Of nature
Ca: And

Brahman's nature is undivided
and absolute, reaffirming its non-dual essence.

4.4.22 (555) – सम्यग्दर्शनात् इति च (Samyagdarśanāt Iti Ca)

And because of the right vision.

Samyagdarśanāt: Due to the right vision
Iti: Thus
Ca: And

Liberation is attained through true knowledge and realization
of Brahman as the ultimate reality, leading to eternal bliss and freedom.

Made in the USA
Monee, IL
07 July 2026